Lifesaver Lessons™
HOLIDAYS & CELEBRATIONS
GRADE 3

Char

S0-AYO-158

What Are Lifesaver Lessons?

Lifesaver Lessons™ are well-planned, easy-to-implement, curriculum-based lessons. Each lesson contains a complete materials list, step-by-step instructions, a reproducible activity or pattern, and several extension activities.

How Do I Use A Lifesaver Lesson?

Each Lifesaver Lesson™ is designed to decrease your preparation time and increase the amount of quality teaching time with your students. These lessons are great for introducing or reinforcing new concepts. You may want to look through the lessons to see what types of materials to gather. After completing a lesson, be sure to check out the fun-filled extension activities.

What Materials Will I Need?

Most of the materials for each lesson can be easily found in your classroom or school. Check the list of materials below for any items you may need to gather or purchase.

- crayons or colored pencils
- markers
- scissors
- glue
- tape
- stapler
- craft sticks
- construction paper
- drawing paper
- notebook paper
- manipulatives
- hole puncher
- encyclopedias and dictionaries
- index cards
- dice
- rulers
- yarn
- lunch-sized paper bags
- U.S. map
- bulletin-board paper

Project Editor:
Cynthia Holcomb

Writers:
Brenda Dunlap, Cynthia Holcomb, Nicole Iacovazzi,
Lisa James, Kathleen Kopp, Mary Ann Lewis,
Ann Moseley, Patricia Pecuch, Julie Plowman

Artists:
Jennifer Bennett, Cathy Spangler Bruce,
Clevell Harris, Mary Lester, Kimberly Richard, Donna K. Teal

Cover Artist:
Jennifer Bennett

Table Of Contents

©1997 by THE EDUCATION CENTER, INC.
All rights reserved except as here noted.
ISBN #1-56234-186-3

Except as provided for herein, no part of this publication may be reproduced or transmitted in any form or by any means,
electronic or mechanical, including photocopying, recording, or storing in any information storage and retrieval system or
electronic on-line bulletin board, without prior written permission from The Education Center, Inc. Permission is given to the
original purchaser to reproduce patterns and reproducibles for individual classroom use only and not for resale or distribution.
Reproduction for an entire school or school system is prohibited. Please direct written inquiries to The Education Center, Inc.,
P.O. Box 9753, Greensboro, NC 27429-0753. The Education Center®, *The Mailbox*®, Lifesaver Lessons™, and the mailbox/
post/grass logo are trademarks of The Education Center, Inc., and may be the subject of one or more federal trademark
registrations. All other brand or product names are trademarks or registered trademarks of their respective companies. Printed
in the United States of America.

Manufactured in the United States
10 9 8 7 6 5 4 3 2 1 0

Grand Grandparent Poems

*Create a display for National Grandparents Day
with this well-versed activity!*

Skill: Writing an acrostic poem

Estimated Lesson Time: 30 minutes

Teacher Preparation:
1. Duplicate a copy of page 5 for each student.
2. Provide an 8-inch construction-paper square for each student.

Materials:
1 copy of page 5 per student
one 8-inch construction-paper square per student
scissors
crayons
glue
large sheet of bulletin-board paper (optional)

Teacher Reference:
National Grandparents Day is celebrated each year in September. The idea for this holiday started in 1973 with Marian McQuade of West Virginia. Ms. McQuade wrote a letter to her governor asking him to recognize a special day for grandparents. The governor approved of her idea and established Grandparents Day for his state. The senator of West Virginia became interested in the project and proposed a bill to set aside a day to honor all grandparents nationwide. In 1978 the U.S. Senate passed his bill, declaring National Grandparents Day to be observed on the first Sunday after Labor Day.

Introducing The Lesson:

Share the background information on page 3. Tell students that they will be using a special type of poetry to create poems in honor of Grandparents Day. Introduce or review the concept of an acrostic poem, in which the first letter of every line spells out a vertical message. Practice an example of an acrostic with your class; then have each student complete one individually for Grandparents Day.

Steps:

1. Write the word "students" on the board. Ask your children to brainstorm words or phrases that begin with each letter of the word. Record the responses on the board.

2. Distribute a copy of page 5 to each student. Instruct each student to create an acrostic poem using the letters in the word "Grandparents."

3. After students have completed their poems, instruct them to cut on the dotted lines.

4. Have each student glue his poem to the center of his construction-paper square.

5. Have students use crayons to decorate their squares.

6. If desired, arrange the squares ion a large sheet of bulletin-board paper to make a patch work quilt.

7. Display the quilt in the classroom. Refer to the extension ideas on page 6 for suggestions on using the poems and quilt for additional Grandparents Day activities.

G reat
R eady to have fun
A lways smiling
N ice to be with
D rives me to school
P lays checkers
A active
R eads to me
E xcellent
N ice
T errific
S uper

Grand Grandparents Poetry

Create an acrostic poem with the letters of the word below.
Cut on the dotted lines.
Then follow your teacher's directions to complete the project.

How To Extend The Lesson:

• Before each student glues her acrostic poem to the construction-paper square, duplicate a class set of each poem. Have each student compile the set of poems into a book. Help each student address an envelope to send the book to her grandparents for a special keepsake of Grandparents Day.

• Take an individual picture of each student standing by the completed quilt. Have each student glue his picture to a card to send to his grandparents.

• Host a Grandparents Day celebration in your classroom. Invite grandparents to join you in the classroom for a party in their honor. (If a student's grandparents are unable to attend, ask community volunteers to serve as "adopted" grandparents for the event.) Have each student read her poem to the class; then serve punch and cookies. For a final activity, provide several of the books listed below for grandparents to read to their grandchildren.

— *The Berenstain Bears And The Week At Grandma's* by Stan & Jan Berenstain (Random House Books For Young Readers, 1986)
— *Could Be Worse!* by James Stevenson (Greenwillow Books, 1977)
— *A Day's Work* by Eve Bunting (Houghton Mifflin Company, 1994)
— *Grandaddy's Highway* by Harriett Diller (Boyds Mills Press, Inc.; 1993)
— *Grandpa's Face* by Eloise Greenfield (Philomel Books, 1996)
— *Grandmama's Joy* by Eloise Greenfield (Philomel Books, 1980)
— *Grandpa's House* by Harvey Stevenson (Hyperion Books For Children, 1994)
— *Gus And Grandpa* by Claudia Mills (Farrar, Straus & Giroux, Inc.; 1996)
— *Tanya's Reunion* by Valerie Flournoy (Dial Books For Young Readers, 1995)
— *There's Nothing To Do!* by James Stevenson (Greenwillow Books, 1986)
— *What's Under My Bed?* by James Stevenson (Greenwillow Books, 1983)
— *When I Am Old With You* by Angela Johnson (Orchard Books, 1993)

• Southwe...
• Basin
And Platea...
• Northwes...
Coast
• Plains
• Eastern
Woodlands

Native American Games

Celebrate a tribute to the first Americans with fun and games—
Native American style!

Skill: Learning about Native American games

Estimated Lesson Time: 30 minutes

Teacher Preparation:
1. Duplicate page 9 for each student.
2. Gather the materials listed below.

Materials:
1 copy of page 9 per student
1 craft stick per student
red crayons
a large United States map (optional)

Background Information:

The first observance of Indian American Day was in 1916, on the second Saturday in May. Although each state now recognizes Native American Day, its observance date varies from state to state. The most common day of observance, however, is the fourth Friday in September.

Before the time of Columbus and other European explorers, the Native Americans had settled throughout North America. There were four main regions of settlement. If possible show your students these regions on a United States map.

• The Woodland tribes lived in the area between the Mississippi River and the east coast, bordering the Atlantic Ocean. The natural resources of the area led them to become farmers, woodsmen, and hunters.
• The Plains tribes lived in the area between the Rocky Mountains and the Mississippi River. The natural resources of the area led them to become farmers, fishermen, hunters, and gatherers.
• The Desert tribes lived in what is now the southwestern region of the United States. The natural resources of the area led them to become villagers, farmers, and nomadic hunters.
• The Northwest Coastal tribes lived in the area between the Pacific Ocean and the Rocky Mountains. The natural resources of the area led them to become fishermen, hunters, and gatherers.

Learning about Native American games (7)

Southwest

• Basin
And Plateau
• Northwest
Coast
• Plains
• Eastern
Woodlands

NATIVE AMERICAN DAY

Introducing The Lesson:

Share the Background Information on page 7 with your students. Tell students that in honor of Native American Day, they will play games that were popular with many different Native American tribes.

Steps:

1. Ask students to think about the types of materials that Native American children might have used in their games. Would their games require the use of dice, spinners, cards, or timers? Ask students to think about the materials that were available for creating and playing games. Reinforce that Native American games included materials that were readily available. Game pieces were made from things easily found in nature, such as sticks, nuts, shells, and stones. Although some Native American games required skill and logic, many were simple games of chance.

2. Tell students that they will play games similar to flipping a coin to determine heads or tails. Since Native Americans did not have coins, they used sticks that were specially designed as game pieces. A stick was smoothed and flattened; then each side of the stick was painted or carved to differentiate the two sides.

3. Distribute a craft stick, a red crayon, and a copy of page 9 to each student. Read the information together as a class; then have each student color her stick according to the instructions.

4. Place students in groups of four to play the games described on page 9.

5. Challenge students to complete the Bonus Box activity.

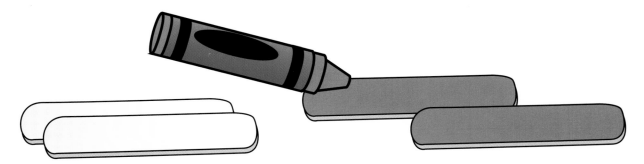

Native American Games

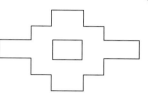

Native American Day is observed the fourth Friday in September. Celebrate this day by playing games that were popular with many Native American tribes. Each game was played with sticks that were smoothed, flattened, and painted red on one side. Prepare a stick to use in the games by coloring one side red. Then get in groups of four to play.

Stick Toss

This was one of the most simple games. Each player uses his own stick.

1. Each player takes a turn tossing his stick in the air. If the stick lands with the red side facing up, the player gets one point.

2. Continue playing until one player earns 20 points. He is declared the winner.

Keep your score here:

Player 1	
Player 2	
Player 3	
Player 4	

Three-Stick Toss

This was one of the most popular stick games played among Native American tribes.

1. Work in teams of two. Use three sticks for this game.

2. Each team takes turns tossing the three sticks on the ground. Points are awarded as follows:

   Three white sides showing—3 points
   Three red sides showing—2 points
   Mixed sides showing—1 point

3. Play continues until one team earns 20 points. That team is declared the winner.

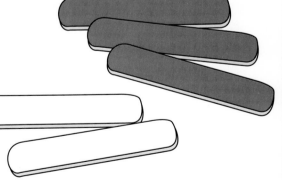

Keep your score here:

Team 1	
Team 2	

Bonus Box: Make up another game using the colored sticks. Write the rules on the back of this paper.

©1997 The Education Center, Inc. • *Lifesaver Lessons*™ • Grade 3 • TEC500

Southwest

• Basin
And Plateau
• Northwest
Coast
• Plains
• Eastern
Woodlands

NATIVE AMERICAN DAY

How To Extend The Lesson:

- Have your students research to find out which Native American tribes lived in your region. Then assign groups of students to find information about the arts and crafts, types of homes, clothing, and shelter of one of the tribes.

- Introduce a variety of Native American cultures to your students. Remind students that not all Native Americans lived in tepees, used bows and arrows, or wore feathered headdresses. Provide resource books so students can compare and contrast tribes such as the Pawnee, the Sioux, the Navajo, the Kickapoo, the Comanche, the Kiowa, the Wichita, the Apache, the Mohawk, and the Ottawa.

- Share these Native American stories with your students:
  —*Coyote And The Firestick: A Northwest Coast Indian Legend* by Barbara Goldin (Harcourt Brace & Company, 1996)
  —*Raven: A Trickster Tale From The Pacific Northwest* by Gerald McDermott (Harcourt Brace & Company, 1993)
  —*Annie And The Old One* by Miska Miles (Little, Brown And Company; 1985)
  —*Arrow To The Sun: A Pueblo Indian Tale* by Gerald McDermott (Viking Children's Books, 1974)
  —*How The Stars Fell Into The Sky* by Jerrie Oughton (Houghton Mifflin Company, 1992)
  —*Iktomi And The Boulder: A Plains Indian Story* by Paul Goble (Orchard Books, 1991)
  —*The Legend Of The Bluebonnet* by Tomie dePaola (G. P. Putnam's Sons, 1996)
  —*The Legend Of The Indian Paintbrush* by Tomie dePaola (G. P. Putnam's Sons, 1988)
  —*Dreamcatcher* by Audrey Osofsky (Orchard Books, 1992)
  —*The Rough-Face Girl* by Rafe Martin (G. P. Putnam's Sons, 1992)

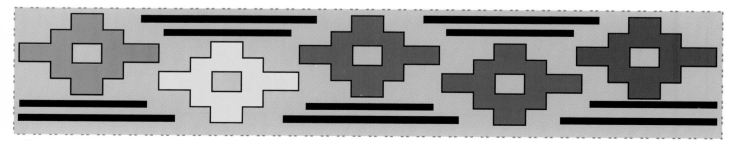

Columbus Day Discoveries

All hands on deck for a Columbus Day writing experience!

Skill: Narrative writing

Estimated Lesson Time: 30 minutes

Teacher Preparation:
Duplicate a copy of page 13 for each student.

Materials:
1 copy of page 13 per student

Background Information:

Christopher Columbus was not the first person to discover America. In fact, he came across it by accident! He was really in search of a faster way to sail to Asia, where the gold and spices of India could be found.

King Ferdinand and Queen Isabella of Spain gave Columbus the money he needed to arrange the voyage. He and his crew set out with three ships on August 3, 1492. The voyage was long and hard. They did not reach land until October 12, when they spotted the Bahamas. Columbus still did not realize that he had landed on a new land. He thought he was close to Japan and China. He named the first island San Salvador.

Columbus did not achieve his original goal of finding a faster trade route to Asia. But by finding a previously unknown continent, Columbus opened the doors to settlement and trade between Europe and America.

Introducing The Lesson:

Tell your students that some of the most important things in history have happened because of mistakes. Remind students that mistakes are not always bad; they can help us learn or show us how to look at things in a new way. Share the Background Information on page 11 with your students. Then have your class discuss the benefits of the historical mistake that Columbus made.

Steps:

1. Explain to students that in addition to finding a new continent, Columbus also found many unfamiliar foods. He and his crew had never seen corn, potatoes, tomatoes, vanilla, beans, pumpkins, avocados, wild rice, chocolate, peppers, pineapples, peanuts, cashews, papayas, pecans, or blueberries before. On the return journey, he brought these foods back to Spain with him.

2. Distribute a copy of page 13 to each student. Instruct students to imagine that they are crew members writing narrative accounts about trying the new foods above. Remind students to describe the appearance, taste, smell, and textures of the new foods.

3. If time allows, have student volunteers read their stories to the class.

_____

by

_____

©1997 The Education Center, Inc. • *Lifesaver Lessons*™ • Grade 3 • TEC500

Note To The Teacher: Use with the writing activity on page 12.

How To Extend The Lesson:

- Explain to students that in addition to finding unfamiliar foods on the new continent, Columbus also introduced foods of European origin to the New World. These foods included peaches, pears, watermelons, olives, bananas, wheat, barley, sugarcane, lettuce, onions, and okra. Divide students into small groups and assign either New World foods or Old World foods to each group. Have each group make a collage or mobile showing the types of foods that were native to each place.

- Use the reproducible on page 13 for Columbus Day reports. Provide reference materials for students to use as they find information about the explorer and his famous voyage.

- Have students reenact Columbus's pleas to the king and queen of Spain for financial support for his voyage. Remind students to be persuasive as they ask for three ships, a crew, and all the supplies and materials needed for the excursion!

- Share these Columbus Day accounts with your students:
  — *In Fourteen Ninety-Two* by Jean Marzollo (Scholastic Inc., 1994)
  — *Christopher Columbus* by Ann McGovern (Scholastic Inc., 1992)
  — *A Picture Book Of Christopher Columbus* by David A. Adler (Holiday House, Inc.; 1991)
  — *Christopher Columbus: Great Explorer* by David A. Adler (Holiday House, Inc.; 1991)
  — *Where Do You Think You're Going, Christopher Columbus?* by Jean Fritz (G. P. Putnam's Sons, 1981)

A Day Of Peace

*Explore the purpose of the United Nations
with a project that promotes the power of peace.*

Skill: Developing vocabulary

Estimated Lesson Time: 30 minutes

Teacher Preparation:
1. Duplicate a copy of page 17 for each student.
2. Gather the supplies listed below.

Materials:
1 copy of page 17 per student
1 sheet of construction paper per student
scissors
crayons
glue

Background Information:
The United Nations first began in 1945 with 51 member nations. Its membership is now approaching the 200 mark. The United Nations organization works to establish world peace, preserve international security, and promote human rights. We celebrate their efforts with a day of recognition on October 24. By observing United Nations Day, students can become aware of the importance of international cooperation and the benefits of world peace.

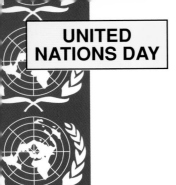

Introducing The Lesson:

Share the Background Information on page 15 with your students. Explain that the United Nations organization sometimes sends troops to an area of conflict. They try to keep the conflict from getting worse while leaders discuss peaceful solutions to their problems. Have students discuss the benefits of using peaceful measures to settle differences.

Steps:

1. Ask students to think of words and phrases that promote peaceful actions. Record their responses on the board. If desired, add words from the list below to the board. Discuss the meaning of each word with your students.

2. Tell students that they are going to use those words and phrases to create a display that celebrates the power of peace. Distribute scissors, crayons, glue, a sheet of construction paper, and a copy of page 17 to each student.

3. Instruct each student to write a word or phrase about peace in each dove on the reproducible. Tell the students to color and cut out each shape; then have them glue the shapes on their construction paper to create a peace collage.

4. Display the completed projects on a bulletin board titled "The Power Of Peace."

The Power Of Peace

respect	cooperation	understanding
fairness	sharing	harmony
patience	helpfulness	kindness
manners	honesty	working together
listening	teamwork	positive thinking
	agreement	compromise
		being responsible

A Day Of Peace

The dove is a symbol of peace.

Write a word or phrase about peace on each dove.

Color and cut out each dove.

Glue the doves to construction paper to make a peace collage.

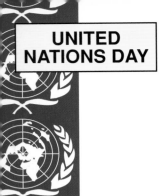
How To Extend The Lesson:

- Have the students list problems that occur frequently in the classroom, on the playground, or when playing with friends at home. Invite students to sit in a circle to discuss peaceful ways of handling each situation.

- Teach students how to say "peace" in different languages. Then have them greet other students and faculty with the multicultural messages.

French	paix	(peh)
German	friede	(FREE duh)
Russian	МИР	(meer)
Spanish	paz	(pahs)
Swahili	amani	(ah MAH nee)
Swedish	fred	(frehd)

- Have each student choose a country that belongs to the United Nations and design that country's flag on a sheet of construction paper as shown. Arrange the completed flags on a bulletin board, or have students display them in a United Nations Day parade around the school grounds.

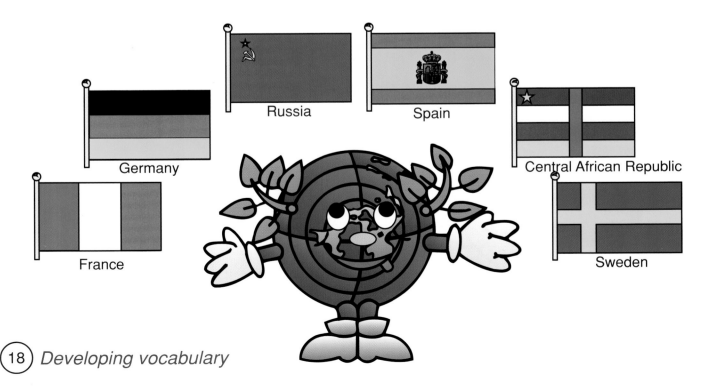

Russia

Spain

Germany

Central African Republic

France

Sweden

"Spook-tacular" Stories

Set the stage for creative writing with a sackful of story elements.

Skills: Reviewing story elements; writing a story

Estimated Lesson Time: 45 minutes

Teacher Preparation:
1. Duplicate a copy of page 21 for each student.
2. Gather the materials listed below.

Materials:
1 copy of page 21 per student
slips of paper
3 paper lunch sacks (or trick-or-treat sacks)
crayons (optional)
drawing paper (optional)

Teacher Reference:
   Halloween may be a time of treats, costumes, and carnivals, but the origins of the holiday had quite a different focus. Many, many years ago, people became frightened as they noticed the long, hot days of summer slowly turning cooler and shorter. The people were afraid that the sun was disappearing and they would be left in darkness. To ward off the evil powers that were causing the sun to leave, the people would burn their crops in huge bonfires. Because the days would eventually become longer and warmer again, the people thought their bonfires and rituals were working. Black cats, witches, and other ghostly creatures also date back to the beliefs of this time period.
   Today we know that the shorter fall days are due to a natural changing of seasons as the earth moves around the sun. Although we still decorate with some of the Halloween symbols of old, the holiday is now known as a fun-filled event for children.

Introducing The Lesson:

Get in the spirit of Halloween by writing some "spook-tacular" stories. Review with students the elements of a story: the characters, the setting, and the plot.

Steps:

1. Have your students brainstorm a list of Halloween story elements while you record the responses on the board. Explain to students that they are going to use items from the list to write hair-raising Halloween tales.

2. Copy the items from the board onto slips of paper. Label each of three paper lunch sacks (or trick-or-treat sacks) with one of the following terms: *character, plot,* or *setting.* Have students assist you in placing each paper in the appropriate sack.

2. Distribute a copy of page 21 to each student.

3. Have each student, in turn, draw two papers from the character sack, one from the setting sack, and one from the plot sack. Instruct the student to use this information to write a Halloween story on the reproducible. Then have the student return the papers to the appropriate sacks.

4. If desired, have each student draw an illustration to go with her story.

5. Provide time for student volunteers to share their stories with the class.

Characters	Settings	Plots
bat	old house	getting lost
jack-o'-lantern	pumpkin patch	finding a broomstick
trick-or-treater	carnival	meeting a monster
spider	forest	eating too much candy
black cat	cave	making a costume

Reviewing story elements

Name_____

_____

by

_____

_____

_____

_____

_____

_____

_____

_____

_____

_____

_____

_____

©1997 The Education Center, Inc. • *Lifesaver Lessons*™ • Grade 3 • TEC500

Note To The Teacher: Use with the activity on page 20.

How To Extend The Lesson:

- Have students work in small groups to write and perform a play. Have each group member draw a paper from the character sack to determine his role in the play. Then have each group draw from the setting sack to determine the setting for their play. Encourage students to create costumes at home to wear during their performance for the class.

- Use the story-element sacks for a guessing game that will promote descriptive writing skills. Have each student draw a paper from one bag to select a topic. Then have each student write a descriptive paragraph about the topic without mentioning it by name. Provide time for each student to share his paragraph with the class and have his classmates identify the topic.

- Treat your students to the following Halloween literature:

  —*Arthur's Halloween* by Marc Brown (Little, Brown & Company; 1996)
  —*Scary, Scary Halloween* by Eve Bunting (Houghton Mifflin Company, 1986)
  —*The Biggest Pumpkin Ever* by Stephen Kroll (Holiday House, Inc.; 1984)
  —*Too Much Trick-Or-Treat* by Jayne Miller (Landmark Editions, Inc.; 1991)
  —*The Ghost With The Halloween Hiccups* by Stephen Mooser (Avon Books, 1978)

Let's Talk Turkey

Use these fine-feathered facts and opinions to reinforce language skills.

Skill: Identifying fact and opinion

Estimated Lesson Time: 30 minutes

Teacher Preparation:
1. Duplicate page 25 for each student.
2. Duplicate the fact-and-opinion statements on page 24 (or copy the sentences on individual strips of paper).

Materials:
1 copy of page 25 per student
1 set of fact-and-opinion strips (See page 24.)
crayons

Teacher Reference:
The first American Thanksgiving was celebrated in 1621. About 50 Pilgrims from the Plymouth colony and 90 Native Americans celebrated and gave thanks for a bountiful harvest. Wild turkey was the main course, and it was probably accompanied by pumpkins, squash, cranberries, and corn.

And speaking of turkey…share these facts with your students:

- Male turkeys are called *toms*.
- Female turkeys are called *hens*.
- Young turkeys are called *poults*.
- Turkeys were first domesticated in Mexico.
- Benjamin Franklin wanted the turkey, not the eagle, to be our national bird.
- There are both wild and domesticated turkeys in North America.

Introducing The Lesson:

Share the information on page 23 with your students. Tell them that they are going to talk turkey to practice fact-and-opinion skills. Ask students to recall the difference between facts and opinions. Then divide students into pairs to practice identifying each type of statement.

Steps:

1. Distribute a strip with one of the statements below to each student pair. Instruct each pair to read the statement, then determine whether it is a fact or an opinion.

2. Have all student pairs with opinion statements move to one side of the room, and all pairs with fact statements move to the other side of the room.

3. Ask each pair to read its statement to the class. Ask the class to decide if the pair correctly identified the type of statement.

4. Distribute a copy of page 25 and a supply of crayons to each student.

5. Provide time for students to complete the reproducible; then challenge them to complete the Bonus Box activity.

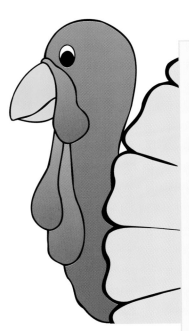

Facts
Turkey is a popular Thanksgiving food.
Pilgrims brought turkeys on the *Mayflower.*
Turkey eggs are twice as big as chicken eggs.
The loose skin on a turkey's throat is called a *wattle.*
Only wild turkeys can fly.
A tom has stiff feathers called a *beard* on his breast.

Opinions
Turkey is good with gravy on it.
Dark meat tastes better than white meat.
Turkeys have prettier feathers than chickens.
Turkeys make a scary noise.
A turkey would make a good pet.
Wild turkeys are nice-looking.

Let's Talk Turkey!

If the statement is a fact, color the feather red.
If the statement is an opinion, color the feather orange.

1. Turkeys are members of the bird family.
2. The adult male wild turkey is about four feet long.
3. Turkeys have beautiful feathers.
4. Everyone enjoys turkey for Thanksgiving.
5. Leftover turkey makes delicious sandwiches.
6. Wild turkeys eat acorns, seeds, berries, and insects.
7. Turkey hens lay from 11 to 20 eggs at a time.
8. Turkeys are fun to raise.
9. They are the most interesting of all birds.
10. We should serve turkey on Valentine's Day, too.
11. Wild turkeys rest in trees at night.
12. It takes about four weeks for a turkey egg to hatch.

Bonus Box: Color the rest of the turkey. On the back of this paper, name this turkey and list three opinions it might have about Thanksgiving.

How To Extend The Lesson:

- Have each student write two paragraphs about her family's Thanksgiving traditions. Challenge students to use only facts in the first paragraph, and only opinions in the second paragraph.

- Play Turkey-Tac-Toe with your students. Draw a tic-tac-toe grid on the chalkboard. Duplicate a supply of the feather patterns below, six on red paper and six on orange paper. Divide the class into two teams and supply each team with one set of colored feathers. Read a fact-or-opinion statement to the first player on the red-feather team. If the student correctly identifies the type of statement, he tapes one of his team's feathers on the grid. Repeat the procedure, alternating teams after each statement is read.

- Share some of these turkey-time tales with your students:
  —*The First Thanksgiving* by Jean Craighead George (Philomel Books, 1993)
  —*A Turkey For Thanksgiving* by Eve Bunting (Houghton Mifflin Company, 1991)
  —*Thanksgiving Day* by Gail Gibbons (Holiday House, Inc.; 1983)
  —*'Twas The Night Before Thanksgiving* by Dav Pilkey (Orchard Books, 1990)
  —*Arthur's Thanksgiving* by Marc Brown (Little, Brown & Company; 1983)
  —*A Visit To Grandma's* by Nancy Carlson (Puffin Books, 1993)

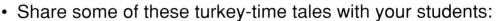

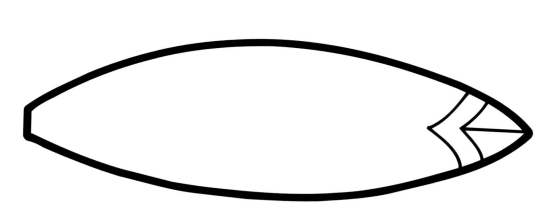

©1997 The Education Center, Inc. • *Lifesaver Lessons*™ • Grade 3 • TEC500 • Key p. 95

The Dreidel Game

Put a spin on Hanukkah festivities with a game that is really tops!

Skill: Learning about Hanukkah traditions

Estimated Lesson Time: 30 minutes

Teacher Preparation:
1. Duplicate a copy of page 29 for each student.
2. Provide ten game tokens—such as nuts, raisins, or pennies—for each student.

Materials:
1 copy of page 29 per student
10 game tokens per student
scissors
glue

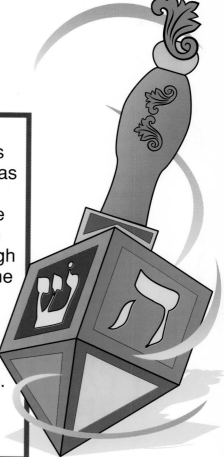

Background Information:
Hanukkah is an eight-day celebration that commemorates the victory of the Jews over the Syrian-Greek invasion. Judas Maccabee led a small army of Jews to defeat the Syrian-Greeks, who had taken over the Jews' holy places. After the victory, the temple in Jerusalem was rededicated. The lamp in the temple was refilled with oil—but there was only enough to keep it lit for a day. A miracle happened, however, and the lamp continued to burn for eight days.

During each night of Hanukkah, a candle is placed in a special candleholder called a *menorah.* A candle is lit every night of the celebration. There are also special games, songs, and gifts that make the holiday a joyous one. One of the traditional games is played with a special top called a *dreidel.*

Introducing The Lesson:

Share the Background Information on page 27 with your students. Explain that during the Hanukkah celebration, children play a game with a special four-sided top called a dreidel. The game is played as follows:

Each player starts out with ten game tokens.
Every player puts one token into the center to make a "pot."
Each player takes a turn spinning the dreidel.
The side of the dreidel facing up after the spin will tell the player to collect from the pot, place tokens in the pot, or do nothing during his turn.

Steps:

1. Distribute a copy of page 29 to each student. Tell students that the Hebrew letters on the dreidel stand for the following directions:

    Nun—*Nothing.* The player passes the dreidel to the next player.
    Gimmel—*All.* The player takes everything in the pot.
    Hey—*Half.* The player takes half of the pot. (If there is an odd number in the pot, the player takes half plus one.)
    Shin—*Put in.* The player puts two tokens in the pot.

2. Instruct students to cut out the dreidel pattern and assemble it to make a top.

3. Place students in groups of three or four. Distribute ten game tokens to each student. Remind each student to put one game token into the pot to start the game. In addition, if only one token (or none) is left in the pot after a turn, every player must add one token to the pot.

4. Provide time for students to play until one player in each group wins all the tokens.

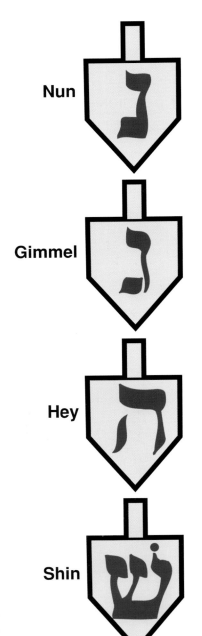

Nun

Gimmel

Hey

Shin

Make A Dreidel

To assemble the dreidel:
1. Cut on the solid black lines.
2. Punch a hole through each circle.
3. Fold on the dotted lines.
4. Fold the pattern to create a cube.
5. Glue down each flap.
6. Insert a pencil through both holes as shown.

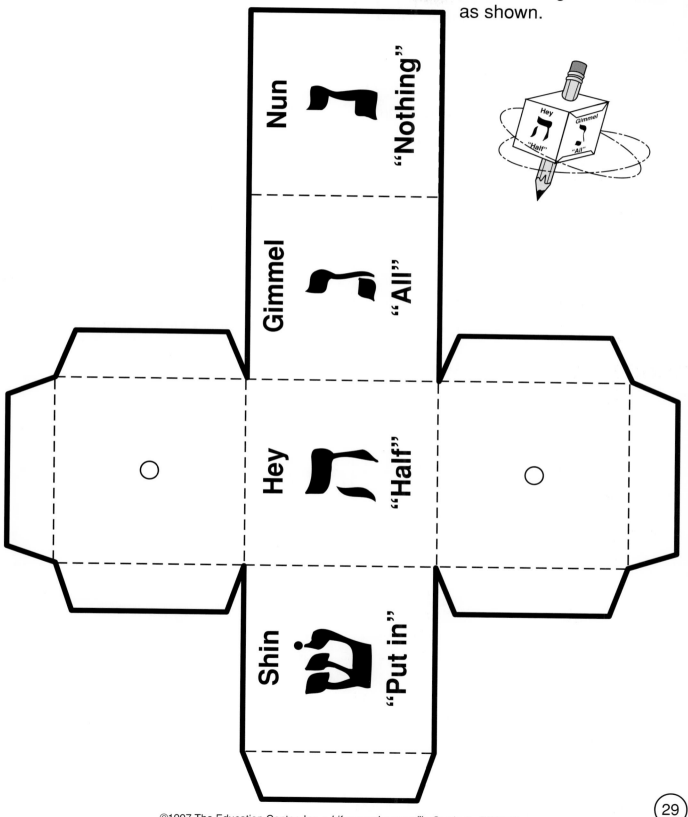

How To Extend The Lesson:

- Have students play a variation on the dreidel game by assigning points to each letter as follows:

  Nun—50 points
  Gimmel—30 points
  Hey—5 points
  Shin—200 points

  Have students play until one player reaches 1,000 points.

- Invite another class to join your students in playing the dreidel game. Have your students explain the rules of the game to the visitors. Then, after the games are over, reward each player with a Hanukkah *gelt,* or gold coin. A chocolate coin wrapped in gold foil serves as the perfect gelt!

- Consult a calendar to find out when Hanukkah falls during the current year. Duplicate a class supply of the menorah pattern below. Have each student color, cut out, and glue her menorah to a sheet of construction paper. For each day of Hanukkah, have each student cut a construction-paper candle to add to her menorah.

Pattern

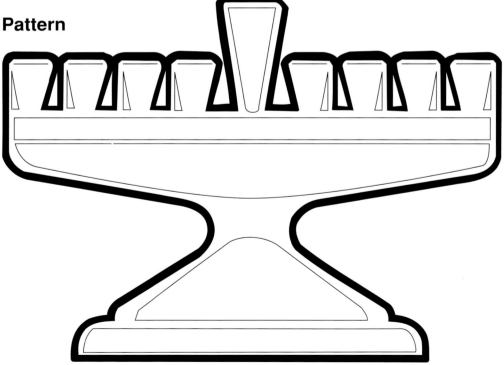

©1997 The Education Center, Inc. • *Lifesaver Lessons*™ • Grade 3 • TEC500

Holiday Plurals

Deck the halls with plural nouns!

Skill: Forming plurals with *s* and *es*

Estimated Lesson Time: 30 minutes

Teacher Preparation:
1. Duplicate a copy of page 33 for each student.
2. Program a set of index cards with words from the lists below.
3. Gather the materials listed below.

Materials:
1 copy of page 33 per student
1 craft stick (or pencil) per student
one 4" x 5" square of red construction paper per student
one 4" x 5" square of green construction paper per student
tagboard tree templates made from the patterns on page 34
programmed index cards
scissors
glue

Teacher Reference:
Most nouns are made plural by adding the suffix *s*.
Most nouns that end in *s, x, z, ch*, or *sh* are made plural by adding the suffix *es*.

Add *s* to form the plurals of these words:
angel
bell
bow
candle
gift
light
ribbon
sled
stocking
tree

Add *es* to form the plurals of these words:
branch
box
bunch
church
dish
dress
glass
kiss
match
wish

Introducing The Lesson:

Tell students that they are going to practice making plural words from a list of holiday vocabulary. For guided practice, each student will make a Christmas tree flasher to review the rules for forming plurals.

Steps:

1. Distribute a craft stick (or pencil), a red and a green square of construction paper, scissors, and glue to each student. Also provide tagboard copies of the tree pattern on page 34 for students to trace.

2. Instruct each student to trace the pattern onto both construction-paper pieces. Tell each student to write "s" on the green tree and "es" on the red tree. Then have the student cut out the tree shapes, place a craft stick (or pencil) between them, and glue them together as shown below to make a Christmas tree "flasher."

3. As the glue dries, review the rules for using *s* and *es* with your students. (See page 31.)

4. Use the set of programmed index cards for guided practice. Hold up each card. Have each student use his Christmas tree flasher to display the correct suffix for forming a plural of the word.

5. After guided practice, distribute a copy of page 33 to each student.

6. Provide time for students to finish the reproducible independently; then challenge them to complete the Bonus Box activity.

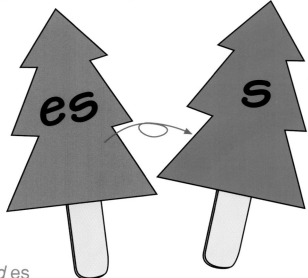

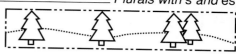

Holiday Plurals

Use *s* or *es* to form a plural of each word in the boxes.
Then use the words to complete each sentence.

1. | ribbon___ |
   | box___ |

   All the _____ were tied with _____ .

2. | candle___ |
   | match___ |

   We used _____ to light the _____ .

3. | toy___ |
   | wish___ |

   The children wrote down their _____ for many new _____ .

4. | light___ |
   | inch___ |

   We have a string of _____ that is 100 _____ long!

5. | bench___ |
   | skate___ |

   After we played on the ice, we sat on the _____ to take off
   our _____ .

6. | branch___ |
   | tree___ |

   Beautiful ornaments hang from the _____ of all the _____ .

7. | bell___ |
   | church___ |

   On Christmas morning, we heard the _____ ringing from the
   _____ in town.

8. | kiss___ |
   | gift___ |

   We gave Grandma many _____ for all the _____ she
   brought us.

9. | patch___ |
   | boot___ |

   As we go caroling, the _____ of snow are slippery under our
   _____ .

10. | glass___ |
    | piece___ |

    We left Santa two _____ of milk and three _____ of pie.

Bonus Box: Choose one of the sentences and draw a picture of it on the back of this paper.

©1997 The Education Center, Inc. • *Lifesaver Lessons*™ • Grade 3 • TEC500 • Key p.95

33

How To Extend The Lesson:

- Use the tree patterns below to make flashers for practice with greater-than and less-than problems, true-and-false statements, fact-and-opinion sentences, and yes-and-no questions.

- Supply students with the lyrics to holiday songs and have them look for plural nouns. "The Twelve Days Of Christmas" provides plenty of plurals!

- Cover three shoeboxes with holiday wrapping paper and ribbon to resemble presents. Program a gift tag for each box, one with *s*, one with *es*, and one with *other plurals*. Cut a slit in each box and place a supply of index cards nearby. Instruct students to write down holiday vocabulary plurals on the cards and deposit each card in the correct box. After a designated time period, open the boxes and have students decide if each word is in the correct box.

Patterns

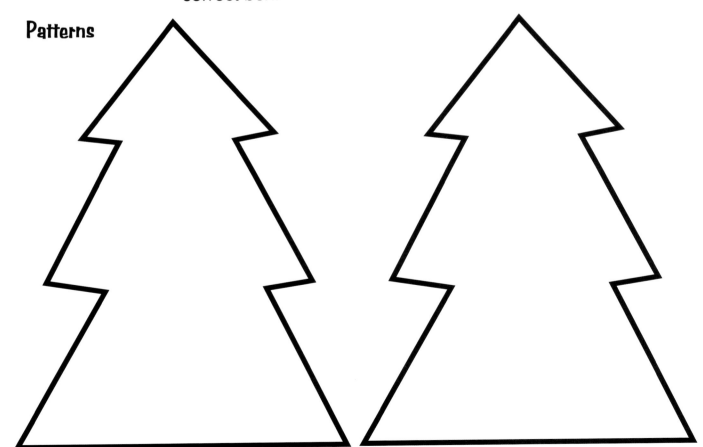

©1997 The Education Center, Inc. • *Lifesaver Lessons*™ • Grade 3 • TEC500

Kwanzaa Lights

Celebrate the lights of Kwanzaa while reinforcing its seven important principles.

Skill: Learning about Kwanzaa customs

Estimated Lesson Time: 45 minutes

Teacher Preparation:
1. Duplicate a copy of page 37 for each student.
2. Write the seven principles of Kwanzaa on the board. (See below.)
3. Gather the materials listed below.

Materials:
1 copy of page 37 per student
1 sheet of yellow construction paper per student
crayons
glue
scissors

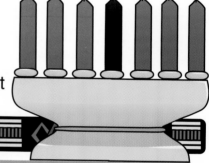

Background Information:
Kwanzaa is a seven-day African-American celebration centered around seven important principles of African customs and values. The celebration takes place each year during the week of December 26 to January 1. A candle is lit during each day of the celebration to highlight one of the principles. Three of the candles in the special candleholder are red to represent past struggles; one candle is black to represent African-American people; and three candles are green to represent the future. The seven principles of Kwanzaa are:

- UMOJA—(oo-MO-jah)—*Unity.* We help each other.
- KUJICHAGULIA—(koo-jee-cha-goo-LEE-ah)—*Self-determination.* We decide things for ourselves.
- UJIMA—(oo-JEE-mah)—*Collective work and responsibility.* We work together to make life better.
- UJAMMA—(oo-jah-MAH)—*Cooperative economics.* We support our community.
- NIA—(NEE-ah)—*Purpose.* We have a reason for living.
- KUUMBA—(koo-OOM-bah)—*Creativity.* We make things with our minds and hands.
- IMANI—(ee-MAH-nee)—*Faith.* We believe in ourselves, our ancestors, and the future.

Introducing The Lesson:

Write the seven principles of Kwanzaa as outlined on page 35 on the board or on a piece of chart paper. Explain to students that each day of Kwanzaa celebrates one of the principles listed on the board. Discuss the meaning of each principle, asking students to think of specific examples that demonstrate each principle.

Steps:

1. Explain to students that a candle is lit during each of the seven nights of Kwanzaa to highlight one of the principles. The candles are placed in a special holder called a *kinara*. The three candles to the left are red to represent past struggles, the middle candle is black to represent the people, and the three candles on the right are green to represent the future.

2. Tell students that they will make models of kinaras that show the seven principles. Distribute scissors, crayons, glue, a sheet of yellow construction paper, and a copy of the reproducible (page 37) to each student.

3. Instruct each student to write one of the principles on each candle, then color the candles the appropriate colors, making sure not to obscure the words.

4. Have each student cut out her candles and glue them in a row on her construction paper. Then have her draw a kinara under the candles.

5. Challenge students to complete the Bonus Box activity.

Kwanzaa Lights

Follow your teacher's direction to color the Kwanzaa
   candles.
Then make a *kinara* for the candles.

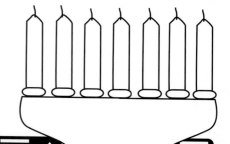

Bonus Box: Draw a picture showing one of the principles of Kwanzaa.

©1997 The Education Center, Inc. • *Lifesaver Lessons*™ • Grade 3 • TEC500

How To Extend The Lesson:

- In addition to Kwanzaa's seven principles, there are seven symbols of the celebration. Two of the symbols are the *mishumaa saba* (mee-SHOO-mah SAH-bah), or Kwanzaa candles; and the *kinara* (kee-NAH-rah), or candleholder, described in the lesson. Introduce your students to the other five symbols:

  —The *mkeka* (mm-KEH-kah) is a woven placemat, a symbol of history.
  —The *kikombe cha umoja* (kee-KOH-beh chah oo-MOH-jah) is a large cup that symbolizes staying together.
  —The *mazao* (mah-ZAH-oh) are fruits and vegetables that symbolize the harvest and hard work.
  —The *muhindi* (moo-HIN-dee) are ears of corn, representing the children.
  —The *zawadi* (zah-WAH-dee) are handmade gifts for children given during the celebration.

- Have your students look at home for examples of the items described above. Encourage students to bring the items to school (with parental permission) to decorate the classroom for the Kwanzaa season.

- Encourage *kuumba* (creativity) by having your students make *zawadi* (handmade gifts) for each other. Have each student secretly draw the name of a classmate in a gift exchange. Then provide materials for students to create gifts, such as macaroni necklaces in Kwanzaa colors, to present to their classmates.

- Have each student bring in pieces of *mazao* (fruits and vegetables) on the last day of Kwanzaa. Arrange the pieces on a *mkeka* (woven placemat) and have a classroom feast.

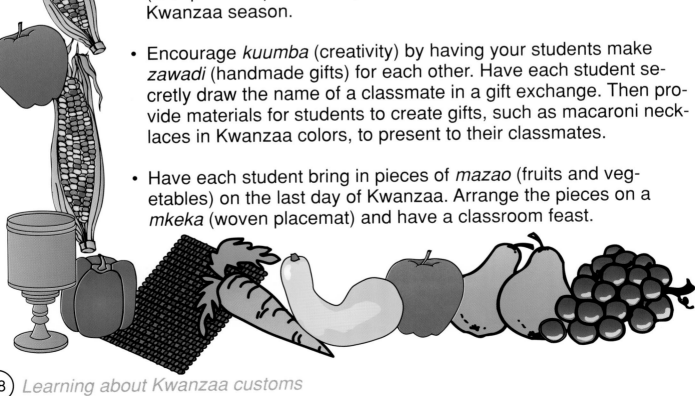

A Gift For The Future

Review the contributions of an American hero as students give their own gifts of thanks.

Skill: Critical thinking; vocabulary development

Estimated Lesson Time: 30 minutes

Teacher Preparation:
1. Duplicate a copy of page 41 for each student.
2. Gather the materials listed below.

Materials:
1 copy of page 41 per student
crayons

Martin Luther King Jr.

Background Information:

Martin Luther King, Jr., was born on January 15, 1929. As a boy, he loved to read and was a very good student. He graduated from college in 1948 and went to Pennsylvania to become a preacher. In 1953 he married Coretta Scott.

In 1954, Martin Luther King became a preacher at a church in Montgomery, Alabama. He received another degree in 1955 and was then called Dr. King. He was dedicated to his belief that all people should be treated equally and decided to use nonviolent ways to make a difference. He led a bus boycott, sit-ins, and protest marches. He also gave many speeches, the most famous of which contained the words, "I have a dream."

In January of 1964, Dr. King was named *Time* magazine's Man Of The Year. In December of the same year, he was awarded the Nobel Peace Prize. As a result of his work, Congress made new laws for equality.

In 1968, while he was planning a multiracial march in Tennessee for antipoverty legislation, Dr. King was fatally shot.

Introducing The Lesson:

Tell students that January 15 is the birthday of a famous civil rights leader, Dr. Martin Luther King, Jr. Share the Background Information on page 39 and the terms below with your students. Explain to your students that during his life, Dr. King gave people many "gifts" that would help future generations. Some of these gifts include teaching people to deal with problems in nonviolent ways, promoting equal rights for everyone, and working to help families in poverty.

Steps:

1. Ask students to think of ways that they could help future generations. Encourage answers such as developing new medicines, working for world peace, promoting education, helping children say no to drugs, and preventing homelessness.

2. Distribute a copy of page 41 to each student. Instruct each student to draw a picture showing how she would like to make the world better for future generations. Then have each student write a paragraph telling how her "gift" will help others.

3. If time allows, ask student volunteers to share their paragraphs with the class.

4. Challenge students to complete the Bonus Box activity.

Terms For Discussion:

boycott—The refusal to buy goods or services from a business in a demonstration to bring about change.

civil rights—The rights, guaranteed by law, that people in the United States have to be treated equally regardless of their race, gender, or religious beliefs.

nonviolence—A method of protest in which people do not physically fight for a cause, but rather demonstrate with sit-ins, marches, boycotts, and other peaceful protests.

segregation—The practice of keeping people separated, especially because of their race.

Name _____

A Gift For The Future

Martin Luther King gave the world many gifts. He showed people how to make changes without violence. He worked for equal rights. He worked to help poor people have a better life.

Think of a gift that would make the world a better place. Draw a picture of the gift; then write about it on the lines below.

_____

_____

_____

_____

_____

_____

_____

Bonus Box: Find out three facts about Dr. King. Write them on the back of this paper.

©1997 The Education Center, Inc. • *Lifesaver Lessons*™ • Grade 3 • TEC500

How To Extend The Lesson:

• Ask students to determine what makes a person a positive role model. Record a list of the characteristics the students mention on the board. Then ask each student to silently evaluate the list and determine which characteristics she possesses, and which ones she will strive to attain.

• Have each student trace his hand two times on a sheet of construction paper, then cut out each shape. Use the handprints as a bulletin-board border. Add the title "Working Together For A Better World." Attach the completed copies of the reproducible on page 41 to show off students' work.

• Use the following books to help students learn more about Dr. King and his accomplishments:
—*Happy Birthday, Martin Luther King* by Jean Marzollo (Scholastic Inc., 1993)
—*Happy Birthday, Dr. King!* by Kathryn Jones (Simon & Schuster Books For Young Readers, 1994)
—*Martin Luther King* by Rosemary L. Bray (Greenwillow Books, 1995)
—*Let Freedom Ring: A Ballad Of Martin Luther King, Jr.* by Myra Cohn Livingston (Holiday House, Inc.; 1992)
—*My Dream Of Martin Luther King* by Faith Ringgold (Crown Publishers, Inc.; 1995)

Delightful Dragons

Celebrate the Chinese New Year with dragons, lanterns, and a parade!

Skill: Learning about the Chinese New Year

Estimated Lesson Time: 45 minutes

Teacher Preparation:

1. Duplicate page 45 for each student.
2. Gather the materials listed below.

Materials:

1 copy of page 45 per student
1 sheet of 9" x 12" construction paper per student
scissors
crayons
glue
rulers

Background Information:

Share these facts about the Chinese New Year with your students.

- The Chinese New Year begins with the first new moon of the year, sometime between January 21 and February 19. The celebration lasts for almost a month.

- With the New Year's new moon, everyone in China turns a year older—no matter what the date of his actual birth.

- For the New Year, the children in China receive small red envelopes containing good-luck money.

- Firecrackers and other noisemakers are used to scare off evil spirits.

- During the New Year, the lion dance is performed to scare away evil spirits and bring good luck. During the dance, dancers dressed as lions move to the beat of a drum.

- In the traditional lantern parade, children carry lanterns of all shapes, sizes, and colors. Each lantern has a riddle attached to it. When the parade is over, the lanterns are hung in public so that everyone can enjoy the riddles.

- The dragon is a symbol of goodness and strength. New Year's parades are led by groups of people wearing huge dragon costumes.

Introducing The Lesson:

Tell your students that not all New Year celebrations occur on January 1. Share the Background Information about the Chinese New Year on page 43 with your students. Tell students that they are going to focus on two important Chinese New Year customs: dragons and lanterns.

Steps:

1. Explain to your students that an important part of the New Year's celebration is the lantern parade. The parade takes place when the first full moon of the new year appears. Each lantern has a paper with a three-clue riddle attached to it. The answer to the riddle is on the back of the paper.

2. Tell students that they will be making riddle lanterns to use in a classroom parade. Each lantern will feature a dragon, the symbol of goodness and strength.

3. Distribute a sheet of construction paper, scissors, glue, and a ruler to each student. Have each student construct a lantern as follows:

   • Fold the paper in half lengthwise, so that the fold is facing the student.
   • Place the ruler an inch from the open end and make a horizontal line across the top of the paper.
   • Slide the ruler down below the horizontal line and mark one-inch increments across the paper as shown.
   • At each inch mark, draw a vertical line beginning at the fold and ending at the horizontal line at the top of the paper (see the illustration).
   • Cut on each vertical line, stopping at the horizontal line at the top of the paper.
   • Unfold the paper. Roll it widthwise, overlapping the ends. Glue the ends together.

4. Distribute a copy of page 45 and crayons to each student. Have each student write a three-clue riddle on the dragon's tail (if desired, have students write a riddle about a Chinese New Year tradition). Then have each student color the dragon pieces, cut them out, and glue the pieces to the lantern.

5. Have students march around the classroom, weaving around the desks, for a lantern parade.

6. After the parade, have students share their riddles before you hang the lanterns as a colorful display.

Name _____

Delightful Dragons

Write a riddle on the dragon's tail.
  Write three clues on the front of the tail.
  Write the answer on the back.
Then color the dragon pieces, cut them out, and glue them to your lantern.

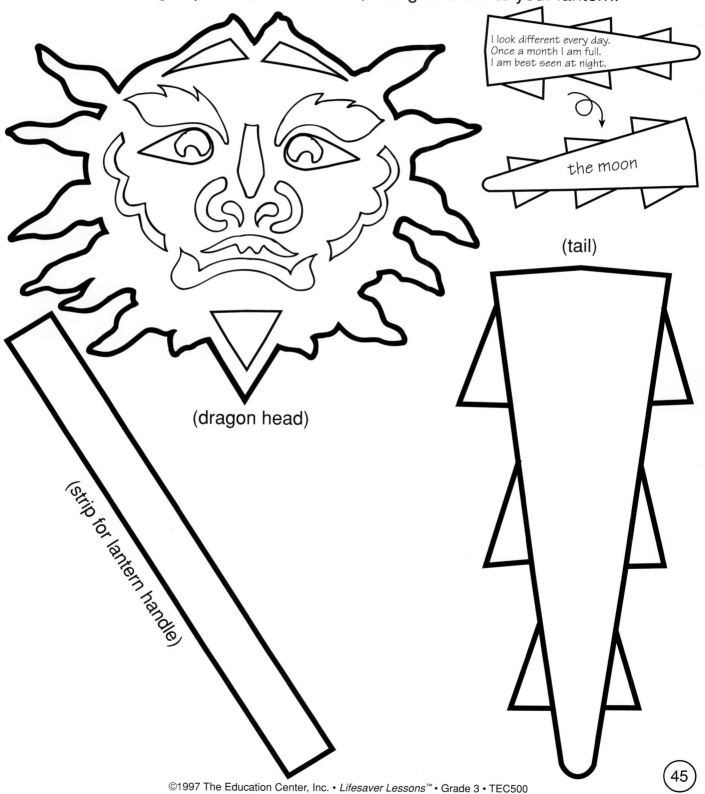

I look different every day.
Once a month I am full.
I am best seen at night.

the moon

(tail)

(dragon head)

(strip for lantern handle)

©1997 The Education Center, Inc. • *Lifesaver Lessons*™ • Grade 3 • TEC500

How To Extend The Lesson:

- To welcome the New Year, the Chinese display banners expressing good luck, best wishes, or thoughts of happiness. The messages are written in couplets on red scrolls and are decorated with flecks of gold. Have your students create banners with red construction paper and gold glitter to hang in the classroom.

- The Chinese display money trees during the New Year in hopes of bringing material prosperity. The trees are fashioned from cypress or pine branches. Garlands made from seeds and nuts are draped over the branches; then the tree is decorated with flowers and money. Bring a large branch into the classroom, and secure it in a vase or flowerpot. Then have your students make decorations to create a money tree for your classroom.

- In China, each new year bears the name of a designated animal. People born under a given animal's year are supposed to possess the distinct characteristics of that animal. Use the chart below to have students determine the animals of their birth years, as well as the animal of the current new year.

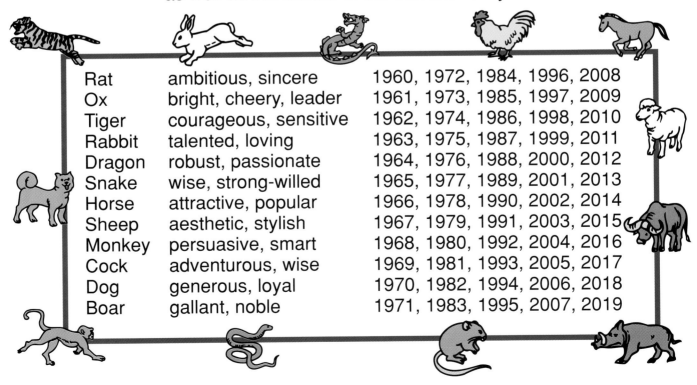

Rat	ambitious, sincere	1960, 1972, 1984, 1996, 2008
Ox	bright, cheery, leader	1961, 1973, 1985, 1997, 2009
Tiger	courageous, sensitive	1962, 1974, 1986, 1998, 2010
Rabbit	talented, loving	1963, 1975, 1987, 1999, 2011
Dragon	robust, passionate	1964, 1976, 1988, 2000, 2012
Snake	wise, strong-willed	1965, 1977, 1989, 2001, 2013
Horse	attractive, popular	1966, 1978, 1990, 2002, 2014
Sheep	aesthetic, stylish	1967, 1979, 1991, 2003, 2015
Monkey	persuasive, smart	1968, 1980, 1992, 2004, 2016
Cock	adventurous, wise	1969, 1981, 1993, 2005, 2017
Dog	generous, loyal	1970, 1982, 1994, 2006, 2018
Boar	gallant, noble	1971, 1983, 1995, 2007, 2019

Valentine Verbs

Put some heart into an activity that reviews action verbs.

Skill: Identifying action verbs

Estimated Lesson Time: 30 minutes

Teacher Preparation:
1. Duplicate page 49 for each student.
2. Write a list of 20 words (10 action verbs, 10 other words) on the chalkboard. (See the example shown on page 48.)

Materials:
1 copy of page 49 per student

Background Information:
One of the most popular Valentine's Day symbols is that of Cupid. He is often portrayed as a winged little boy carrying a bow and arrows. In ancient Roman mythology, Cupid was the god of love. The Romans believed that when Cupid shot an arrow at someone's heart, the person would fall in love with whomever he was looking at. Cupid was a bit of a prankster, though, and would sometimes cause someone to fall in love with the wrong person!

Introducing The Lesson:

Tell students that they will need to put a lot of heart into their work today. Share the information about Cupid on page 48. Tell students that they are going to help Cupid identify some action verbs. Review with your students the fact that an action verb shows the activity of the subject. Tell students to look at the list of words on the board and identify which words are action verbs.

Steps:

1. Call on a student volunteer to identify an action word from the list. If he is correct, have him draw a heart around the word.

2. Continue calling on volunteers until the ten words have been identified.

3. Challenge students to use each verb in a sentence. Call on different volunteers to create sentences from the verbs on the board. After a word has been used in a sentence, have that volunteer draw an arrow through the heart.

4. Distribute a copy of page 49 to each student.

5. Provide time for students to complete the reproducible; then challenge them to complete the Bonus Box activity.

Valentine Verbs

Next to each letter, write an action verb that begins with that letter.
Then write a sentence using each verb.

H _____ _____.

E _____ _____.

A _____ _____.

R _____ _____.

T _____ _____.

L _____ _____.

A _____ _____.

C _____ _____.

E _____ _____.

R _____ _____.

E _____ _____.

D _____ _____.

Bonus Box: On another sheet of paper, design a valentine card. Write a message that contains two verbs.

49

©1997 The Education Center, Inc. • *Lifesaver Lessons*™ • Grade 3 • TEC500

How To Extend The Lesson:

• Purchase a box of valentine cards and place the cards in a learning center. Challenge students to read each card and find the verbs in the message. Program the backs of the cards for self-checking.

• Duplicate copies of the Cupid pattern below. Program each pattern with a verb and store the patterns in an envelope. Instruct each student to randomly select three verbs from the envelope and write a paragraph using all three verbs.

• Share the love of books with your students with these Valentine's Day favorites:
— *Arthur's Valentine* by Marc Brown (Little, Brown & Company; 1980)
— *Louanne Pig In The Mysterious Valentine* by Nancy Carlson (Puffin Books, 1987)
— *Two Hundred Thirteen Valentines* by Barbara Cohen (Henry Holt & Company, Inc.; 1993)
— *The Red, White, And Blue Valentine* by Patricia Reilly Giff (Dell Books For Young Readers, 1993)
— *Horrible Harry And The Kickball Wedding* by Suzy Kline (Viking Children's Books, 1992)

Identifying action verbs

©1997 The Education Center, Inc. • *Lifesaver Lessons*™ • Grade 3 • TEC500

Presidential Profiles

Capitalize on chart-reading skills with a wealth of presidential information.

Skill: Reading a chart

Estimated Lesson Time: 30 minutes

Teacher Preparation:
Duplicate a copy of page 53 for each student.

Materials:
1 copy of page 53 per student

Teacher Reference:
Presidents' Day was originally declared to celebrate the birthdays of Presidents George Washington (born February 22, 1732) and Abraham Lincoln (born February 12, 1809). President Washington is best remembered for being the first president and the "father of our country." President Lincoln, our 16th president, is known for his strong leadership during the Civil War years and for freeing the slaves. As we pay tribute to both men on the third Monday in February, it is also a time to honor all the presidents of the United States.

Share some unusual information about past presidents with your students. Here are a few interesting bits of trivia:
— Thomas Jefferson preferred to wear his farming clothes.
— John Quincy Adams bathed in the Potomac River every morning.
— Zachary Taylor was famous for never missing a spittoon when he spat his chewing tobacco.
— Andrew Johnson was sold at the age of 14 to become a tailor's servant.
— William Taft was so large that he once became stuck in a bathtub.
— Gerald Ford was offered tryouts by two professional football teams.

(For other interesting tidbits, as well as biographical information, refer to the book *Wooden Teeth And Jelly Beans* by Ray Nelson, Douglas Kelly, Ben Adams, and Mike McLane [Beyond Words Publishing, Inc.; 1995].)

Introducing The Lesson:

Spark students' interest in Presidents' Day by sharing the information on page 51. Then inform students that the role of president includes some very important jobs (refer to the information below). Explain that our nation has been led by some great (and not-so-great) presidents. Each president is rated on what he accomplishes while in office. If people believe the president's actions are good for the nation, he is considered an effective and popular president. Abraham Lincoln is the only president in our nation's history so far that historians recognize as being "truly great." George Washington was rated as "great," largely because of the responsibilities he had as our first president.

Steps:

1. Tell students that they will use a chart to find information about several presidents' time in office.

2. Distribute a copy of page 53 to each student.

3. Provide time for students to answer the questions on the reproducible; then challenge them to complete the Bonus Box activity.

Some of the president's roles include:
—**Chief Executive** The president enforces federal laws and treaties, develops federal policies, prepares the national budget, and appoints federal officials.
—**Commander In Chief** The president serves as the commander of the armed services to defend the country during war, and to keep it strong during peacetime.
—**Foreign Policy Director** The president has the power to appoint ambassadors, make treaties, and receive foreign diplomats.
—**Party Head** The president helps form the party's position regarding important issues.
—**Popular Leader** The president makes decisions for the entire nation ahead of those of any state or citizen.
—**Chief Of State** The president participates in national events, such as dedications to national parks, throwing out the first baseball of the season, and attending historic celebrations.

Name _____

Presidential Profiles

Use the chart to help answer the questions.

President	Order In Presidency	Time In Office	Accomplishments	Rating
George Washington	1st	1789–97	He held the nation together during its early days and helped form the nation.	Great
James Madison	4th	1809–17	He allowed the country to become involved in an unnecessary war, but then quickly made peace.	Average
John Tyler	10th	1841–45	He declared that the vice president would take over in the event of the president's death.	Below Average
Abraham Lincoln	16th	1861–65	He held the nation together during a difficult time in history; helped put an end to slavery.	Truly Great
Theodore Roosevelt	26th	1901–9	He worked to establish national parks and forests, and the Panama Canal.	Near Great
Dwight Eisenhower	34th	1953–61	He ended the war in Korea.	Average

1. Who was in office in 1861?

2. Which president was considered "near great"?

3. Who was the tenth president?

4. Who helped establish the Panama Canal?

5. Which two presidents were considered "average"?

6. How long was Theodore Roosevelt president?

7. Which president received the lowest rating?

8. Which two presidents are credited for helping the nation stay together?

9. What order in the presidency was President Lincoln?

10. What years did President Eisenhower serve as president?

Bonus Box: How would you rate your schoolwork? Use the presidential rating scale for your answer.

53

How To Extend The Lesson:

- Assign groups of students to research different presidents. After compiling biographical facts about a president, have each group present the information to the class as a television program.

- Have each student write an essay describing what he would do if he were president. Start with a brainstorming session to have students identify matters that the president should address. Then have each student describe his opinions and intentions for these matters. Compile the completed essays in a classroom newspaper.

- Inform students that in order to become president of the United States, a person must be at least 35 years old, be a natural-born citizen, and have lived in the United States for at least 14 years. Have students discuss these qualifications. Then have them decide why a presidential candidate must meet each of those guidelines.

- Hold an election for class president. Have each student who wishes to run for the office write a campaign speech to deliver in front of the class. Ask each candidate to address her position on such issues as classroom rules, playground behavior, and homework policies. Then have your students use copies of the ballot slip below to vote for their favorite candidates.

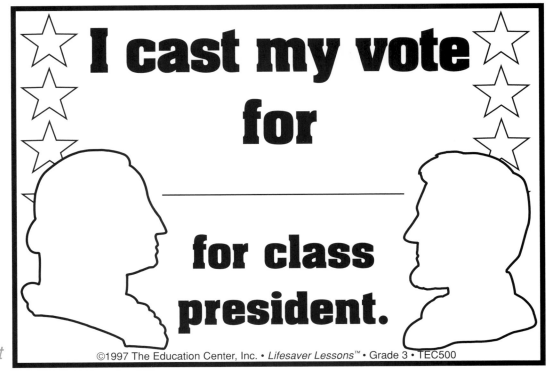

I cast my vote for _____ for class president.

©1997 The Education Center, Inc. • *Lifesaver Lessons*™ • Grade 3 • TEC500

Pot O' Gold

Challenge your students with a game that combines the luck of the Irish and problem-solving strategies.

Skills: Using problem-solving strategies; adding money to $1.00

Estimated Lesson Time: 30 minutes

Teacher Preparation:
1. Duplicate a copy of page 57 for each student pair.
2. Duplicate a copy of the shamrocks on page 58 on green construction paper for each student pair. (Or, if desired, use another type of manipulative for game pieces.)
3. Gather the materials listed below.

Materials:
1 copy of page 57 per student pair
1 set of shamrocks (page 58) per student pair (or 18 manipulatives per pair)
1 sheet of notebook paper per student pair

Teacher Reference:
A Wee Bit O' Irish Trivia
- St. Patrick's Day honors the man who introduced Christianity to Ireland about 1,550 years ago.

- St. Patrick is believed to have driven all the snakes out of Ireland, and there are no snakes there today.

- Ireland is known as the Emerald Isle because of the lush vegetation. The shamrock clover grows in abundance!

- The potato is a staple of the Irish diet.

- The legend of the leprechaun dates back over 1,550 years. If caught, these little men, who resemble elves, must reveal where a buried treasure lies. The treasure is typically a pot of gold hidden at the end of the rainbow.

Using problem-solving strategies (55)

Introducing The Lesson:

Ask students if they are familiar with the legend of the leprechaun. Use the Teacher Reference on page 55 to share information about the leprechaun (as well as other Irish trivia, if desired) with your students. Then tell students that they are going to work in pairs to play a game with a special pot of gold.

Steps:

1. Place students in pairs. Distribute a copy of page 57, a set of shamrocks (page 58) or manipulatives, and a sheet of notebook paper to each pair.

2. Explain the rules of the game as follows:

> —Each student will receive 9 shamrocks or manipulatives.
> —Student partners will take turns placing a shamrock or manipulative over any *uncovered* coin on the gameboard.
> —When a student covers a coin, she records the value of the coin on the notebook paper. On each of her following turns, she adds the value of the coin she covers to her previous amount.
> —The partner who comes closest to $1.00 without going over is the winner.

Note: A student may wish to "hold" at an amount and forfeit additional turns at any time. However, once she decides to stop covering coins, she may not change her mind during the game.

3. After each pair completes the game, challenge them to complete the Bonus Box activity.

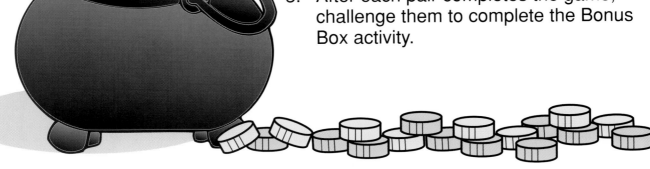

Pot O' Gold!

Take turns covering a coin.
Each time you cover a coin, add its value to your score.
The person who comes closest to $1.00 without going over is the winner.

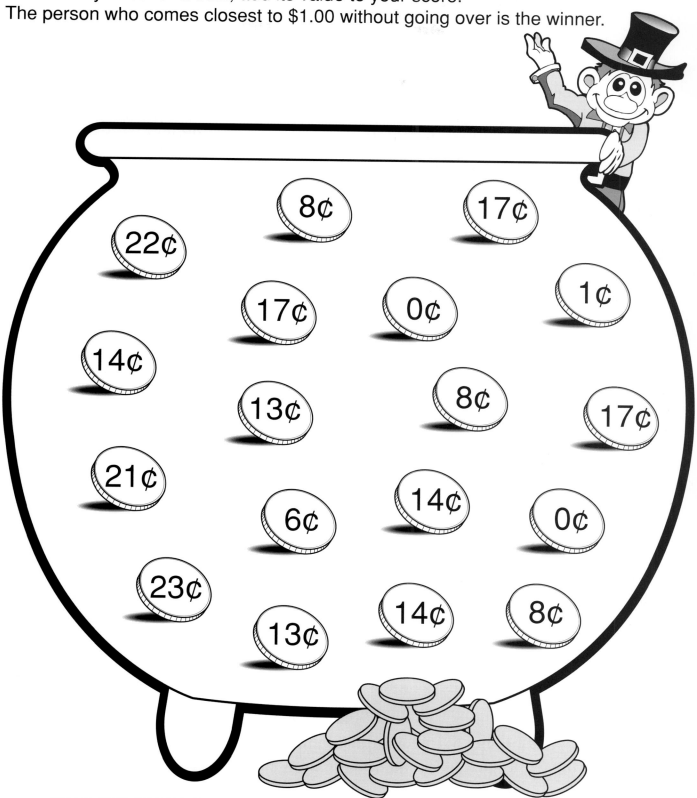

Bonus Box: Play the game starting with a score of $1.00. Subtract the value of each coin as you cover it. The person who has the lowest score at the end of the game wins!

©1997 The Education Center, Inc. • *Lifesaver Lessons™* • Grade 3 • TEC500

How To Extend The Lesson:

- For an added challenge, have student pairs play the game on page 57 following the same rules *except* that the winner must have a score of exactly $1.00.

- Have each student write a story about trying to catch a leprechaun. Tell students to describe the clever ways the leprechaun might try to avoid getting caught.

- Have students use potatoes to make prints. Cut potatoes in half and distribute a half to each student. Provide plastic knives for students to use as they cut the shape of a shamrock into the potatoes. Then supply green tempera paint for students to dip the potatoes in to make prints on white construction paper.

- Celebrate the wearin' o' the green with these tales:
  — *Tim O'Toole And The Wee Folk* by Gerald McDermott (Viking, 1990)
  — *Leprechauns Never Lie* by Lorna Balian (Humbug Books, 1994)
  — *Clever Tom And The Leprechaun* by Linda Shute (Scholastic Inc., 1990)
  — *Seeing Is Believing* by Elizabeth Shub (Greenwillow Books, 1994)
  — *A Treasury Of Irish Stories* chosen by James Riordan (Kingfisher, 1995)

Shamrock Game Pieces
Use with "Pot O' Gold!" on page 57.

©1997 The Education Center, Inc. • *Lifesaver Lessons*™ • Grade 3 • TEC500

The Bunny Hop

This "hare-raising" strategy game will reinforce problem-solving strategies by leaps and bounds!

Skill: Using problem-solving strategies

Estimated Lesson Time: 30 minutes

Teacher Preparation:
1. Duplicate page 61 for each student.
2. Provide 14 jelly beans (or other small manipulatives) for each student.

Materials:
1 copy of page 61 per student
14 jelly beans (or other manipulatives) per student

Teacher Reference:
Share these remarkable rabbit facts with your students.

- A wild rabbit named Flopsy was kept as a pet and lived to be 18 years old.

- A show rabbit named Sweet Majestic Star had ears that measured 28 1/2 inches long and 7 1/4 inches wide.

- A domestic rabbit in Spain weighed 26 pounds, 7 ounces.

- The heaviest recorded wild rabbit weighed 8 1/4 pounds. (The average weight for a wild rabbit is only 3 1/2 pounds.)

- The Netherland dwarf and the Polish dwarf breeds weigh only about 2 pounds when fully grown.

- Female rabbits (called *does*) typically have five litters a year. The New Zealand white and Californian breeds have been recorded as having six litters a year with up to 12 babies (called *kittens*) in their litters. Wild rabbits usually have only 3–7 kittens per litter.

- A domestic rabbit in Nova Scotia, Canada, was recorded as having 24 kittens in one litter.

Introducing The Lesson:

Share the rabbit facts on page 59 with your students. Then tell your students that they are going to play a game that will really have them hopping. As they play several rounds of the game, students will see that they must use strategy to make the best possible score.

Steps:

1. Distribute 14 jelly beans (or other manipulatives) and a copy of page 61 to each student.

2. Instruct each student to place a jelly bean on all but one circle. Explain the rules of the game as follows:

   - Students must "jump" one jelly bean at a time diagonally or horizontally over another jelly bean and make it land in an empty circle. (Show students that the lines connecting the circles will help them determine which ways the jelly beans are allowed to jump.)
   - After a jelly bean has been jumped, it is removed from the gameboard.
   - Continue jumping the jelly beans until there are no possible moves to make.
   - Count the number of jelly beans remaining on the gameboard. The lower the score, the better the game!

3. Have each student play a practice round at his desk. Challenge the student to leave only one jelly bean on his board.

4. Place students in groups of two or three. Have each student in turn play one round of the game per turn. Have the student add his score from three rounds to come up with a total. The student in each group with the lowest score is the winner.

5. Challenge students to complete the Bonus Box activity.

The Bunny Hop

Do the Bunny Hop!
Follow your teacher's directions for playing the game.

Bonus Box: Find out the scores for five of your classmates. Make a chart to show the results.

How To Extend The Lesson:

- Take your students outside for a real hopping challenge. Designate two points as the starting line and finish line. Have three students at a time take their place at the starting line. Then, at your signal, the three students hop their way to the finish line. Continue until all students have had a chance to participate, or divide the class into three teams to compete in a relay version of the race.

- After sharing the rabbit facts on page 59 with your students, challenge each student to discover three more facts about rabbits. If desired, duplicate a supply of the rabbit pattern below on which students can record their facts. Then display the fact-filled bunnies on a bulletin board titled "Read About Remarkable Rabbits!"

Pattern

©1997 The Education Center, Inc. • *Lifesaver Lessons*™ • Grade 3 • TEC500

Hooray For Books!

Celebrate the joy of good books as students recall their literary favorites.

Skill: Following directions

Estimated Lesson Time: 45 minutes

Teacher Preparation:
1. Duplicate a copy of page 65 for each student.
2. Gather the materials listed below.

Materials:
1 copy of page 65 per student
1 sheet of construction paper or tagboard per student
scissors
crayons
yarn
glue
hole puncher

Background Information:
International Children's Book Day is held annually on April 2 to commemorate the birthday of Hans Christian Andersen, well-loved author of such fairy tales as *The Ugly Duckling, The Little Mermaid,* and *The Emperor's New Clothes.* The holiday is sponsored by the International Board On Books For Young People, or the IBBY. Each year a different country officially sponsors the event, and every other year the IBBY presents an award to one children's author and one illustrator. This event provides a good springboard for having students recall their favorite stories and books.

Introducing The Lesson:

Tell students that April 2 is the birthday of a famous children's author. Write *Hans Christian Andersen* on the board. Ask students if they can name any of his stories. If not, write a few of his more familiar works on the board, such as *The Ugly Duckling, The Little Mermaid, The Emperor's New Clothes, The Princess And The Pea,* and *Thumbelina.* Have students discuss whether or not they have heard of or enjoyed any of these stories.

Steps:

1. Inform students that International Children's Book Day is celebrated on Mr. Andersen's birthday, and it is sponsored by a different country each year. Every other year, a children's author and illustrator receive the Hans Christian Andersen Award during the celebration.

2. Ask students to name books they think are worthy of winning an award. List their responses on the board.

3. Distribute to each student a copy of page 65, a sheet of construction paper or tagboard, scissors, glue, crayons, and several lengths of yarn. Tell students that they will each make a mobile of a likeness of themselves holding four of their favorite books.

4. Provide time for each student to color his reproducible and glue it to the construction paper before cutting out the patterns. Help each student assemble his mobile as shown. Suspend the finished projects from the ceiling.

Hooray For Books!

Create a mobile with the patterns below.
Show a likeness of yourself holding four of your favorite books.

©1997 The Education Center, Inc. • *Lifesaver Lessons*™ • Grade 3 • TEC500

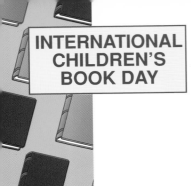
How To Extend The Lesson:

- Fill a crate or plastic tub with classic children's stories, or invite students to bring favorite books from home. Provide a special time for students to select one of the books for independent reading.

- Arrange for your students to pair up with a lower grade for a special story sharing. In advance have each of your students select a book and practice reading it aloud. Then have your students read their selections to younger students on April 2.

- Have students work in small groups to discuss and decide on ten "must reads" for third grade. Provide materials for each group to use to design a poster showing their selections. Display the finished posters in the hallway or library for other students to observe.

- Have each student write a letter to an adult asking him to name his favorite children's book, author, or illustrator. Discuss the responses and locate copies of the books, if possible, for your students to enjoy. If desired invite the adults to come to the classroom and read a story to the class.

- Provide each student with a copy of the bookmark pattern below. Encourage each student to decorate the bookmark with the names of stories, characters, or authors that she has enjoyed. Then help each student punch a hole in the bookmark as indicated and loop a yarn tassel through the opening.

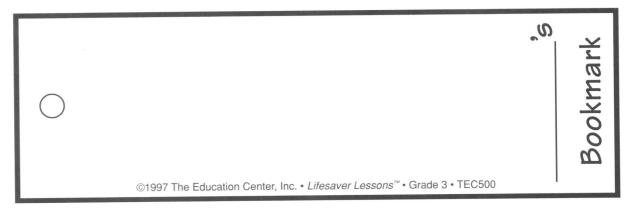

©1997 The Education Center, Inc. • *Lifesaver Lessons*™ • Grade 3 • TEC500

Happy Earth Day!

Review the three Rs of conservation with an Earth Day celebration.

Skill: Reviewing conservation measures

Estimated Lesson Time: 45 minutes

Teacher Preparation:

1. Duplicate the reproducible on page 69 for each student.
2. Gather the materials listed below.

Materials:

1 copy of page 69 per student
one 9-inch square of construction paper per student
crayons
scissors
glue
masking tape

Teacher Reference:

When it comes to conservation, the three *Rs* are *reduce, reuse,* and *recycle.*

Reducing means lessening the amount of trash through wise buying of items with little packaging. Styrofoam® is one item to be reduced since it is not biodegradable and causes problems in landfills.

Reusing means not discarding items after one use; items are used again for the same or another function. Grocery sacks are often reused. After unloading your groceries, you can use the sacks as wastebasket liners or overnight bags, or you can take them with you on your next trip to the grocery store and use them again.

Recycling means passing items through a cycle which reprocesses the materials instead of throwing them away. Aluminum cans are often recycled. After being reprocessed, the aluminum is used again to make new cans.

Introducing The Lesson:

Inform students that April 22 is Earth Day, a special time to think about taking care of our planet. Review the three *R*s of conservation as described in the Teacher Reference on page 67. Then ask students to describe ways to take care of the earth using the three *R*s or other methods.

Steps:

1. Tell students that in celebration of Earth Day, they are going to create a conservation quilt that shows their dedication to taking care of the planet.

2. Distribute a copy of page 69, a square of construction paper, crayons, glue, and scissors to each student.

3. Tell students to complete the reproducible by drawing or writing an idea for taking care of the earth in the box. Then have each student cut out the box and glue it to the center of the construction-paper square.

4. Tape the completed squares together to create a conservation quilt. Display the quilt in the hallway to remind others to be conservation-conscious and earth-friendly!

Name_____

Happy Earth Day!

Draw a picture or write a message about taking care of the earth.
Then follow your teacher's directions for creating a conservation quilt.

©1997 The Education Center, Inc. • *Lifesaver Lessons*™ • Grade 3 • TEC500

How To Extend The Lesson:

• Increase your students' awareness of the many items in their homes and classroom that are often discarded. Have students make a list of these items. Then brainstorm ways to reuse, reduce, or recycle items that are typically thrown away.

• Set up three boxes in your classroom. Label each box with "Reduce," "Reuse," or "Recycle." Encourage students to bring in examples of items to put in each box. Invite students to take objects from the "Reuse" box if they can put them to good use. Arrange for the items in the "Recycle" box to be taken to a recycling center. Then have your students find the best way to discard items in the "Reduce" box, and remind them to be careful of purchasing those items again in the future.

• Have students write acrostic poems with the words *reduce, reuse*, and *recycle*. Challenge them to give earth-friendly suggestions for each letter.

Read packages for the recycle symbol.
Each person should try to reduce waste.
Don't buy aerosol cans.
Use earth-friendly materials.
Caution—Styrofoam® is not biodegradable!
Everybody should help the earth!

Math-Fact Fiesta

Reinforce basic math facts with a Cinco de Mayo celebration.

Skill: Reinforcing addition or multiplication facts

Estimated Lesson Time: 30 minutes

Teacher Preparation:

1. Duplicate a copy of page 73 for each student.
2. Gather the materials listed below.

Materials:

1 copy of page 73 per student
1 sheet of notebook paper per student
1 die per group of three students
crayons (optional)

Background Information:

Share these facts about the Cinco de Mayo celebration with your students.

- Cinco de Mayo (May 5) commemorates the day in 1862 when the Mexican army defeated the invading, well-trained French troops.
- Flowers—both real and made of paper—are displayed on floats, used as decorations, and worn as part of holiday costumes.
- Mariachi bands play lively music throughout the day.
- There are parades that feature people dressed in French and Mexican army uniforms and women with flowery hats.
- After the parades, there are mock battles with cannons, rifles, and sword fights.
- The celebration also includes dancing, barbecues, beauty contests, and political speeches.
- A huge fireworks display concludes the festivities.

Introducing The Lesson:

Tell your students that May 5 marks one of the most important fiesta days in Mexico and in American communities that have a large Mexican-American population. Share the Background Information on page 71 with your students. Then tell students that they will learn to count in Spanish, the native language of Mexico, to practice math facts.

Steps:

1. Write the word *cinco* on the board. Explain that *cinco* is the Spanish word for five. The name of the holiday *Cinco de Mayo* means "the fifth of May."

2. Distribute a sheet of notebook paper and a copy of page 73 to each student. Review the counting chart on page 73 as students orally practice counting to ten in Spanish.

3. Explain to students that they will work in groups of three to create a set of math problems. Each group will have a die and a sheet of notebook paper. The members of the group take turns rolling the die onto their reproducibles. Each member of the group records the number shown on the die and adds it to (or multiplies it by) the number word that the die landed on.

4. The group members take five turns each so that 15 problems are created.

5. Each group member solves the problems independently. When all members are through, they compare answers to check their work.

6. Challenge students to complete the Bonus Box activity.

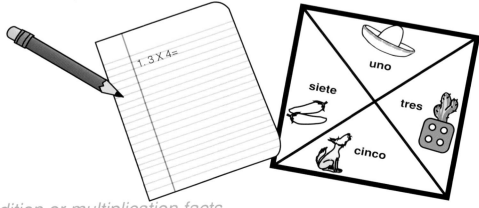

Name _____

Math-Fact Fiesta

Follow your teacher's directions to create a set of math problems.

uno — one	**tres** — three	**cinco** — five	**siete** — seven	**nueve** — nine
dos — two	**cuatro** — four	**seis** — six	**ocho** —eight	**diez** — ten

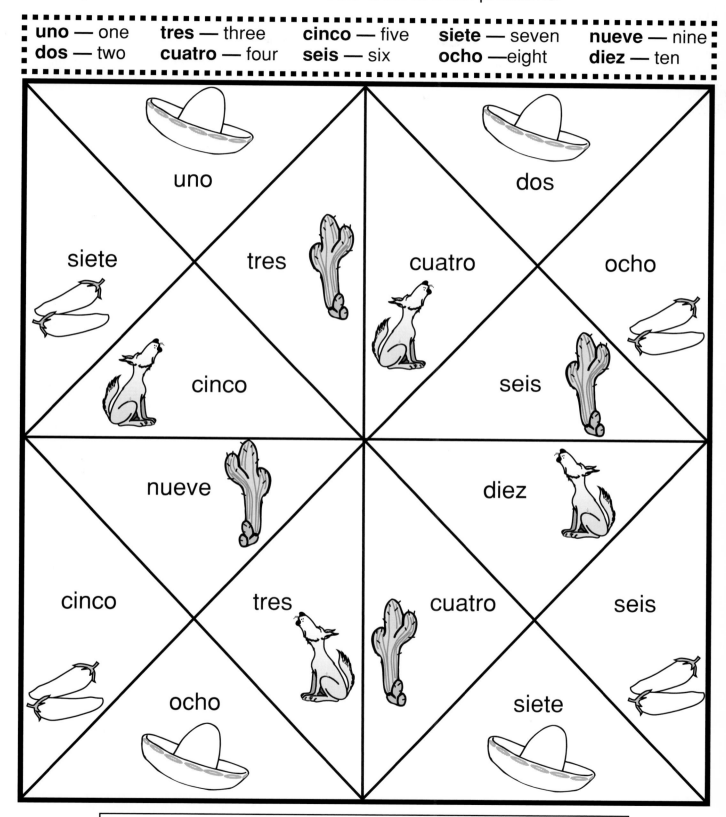

uno

dos

siete

tres

cuatro

ocho

cinco

seis

nueve

diez

cinco

tres

cuatro

seis

ocho

siete

Bonus Box: Write a word problem using the Spanish name for each number in it. Then trade papers with a classmate and solve his or her problem.

©1997 The Education Center, Inc. • *Lifesaver Lessons*™ • Grade 3 • TEC500

How To Extend The Lesson:

- Create a *mariachi* rhythm section in your classroom. Have students make shakers by placing a few dried beans inside empty film canisters; folded and stapled paper plates; or clean, empty milk cartons. Then play recorded Mexican music and have students shake their instruments to the beat.

- Have students locate Mexico on a map. Ask students to identify the states Mexico borders (Texas, New Mexico, Arizona, and California), the bodies of water that surround it (Pacific Ocean and Gulf of Mexico), and its capital (Mexico City).

- Decorate your classroom for Cinco de Mayo with festive flowers. To make a flower, each student will need three coffee filters and a green pipe cleaner. Instruct each student to fold each of his filters into quarters. Supply several containers of water mixed with food coloring. Have each student dip one end of each filter into a container of colored water, letting the filter absorb the color. Then have him unfold the filters and lay them flat to dry.

  When the filters are dry, instruct each student to stack his filters on top of one another. Tell the student to place his finger in the center of the top filter and gather the stack up around his finger. Then have him secure the flower with a pipe-cleaner stem. Staple the completed flowers to a bulletin board or display the colorful creations around the classroom.

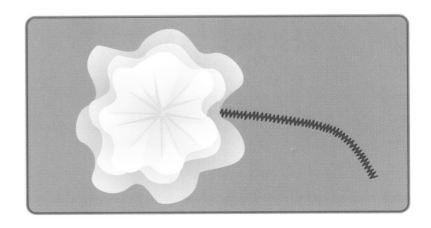

Brilliant Blooms For Mother's Day

Observe the traditions of Mother's Day with a graphing activity and a flower-filled card.

Skills: Reading a bar graph; making a card

Estimated Lesson Time: 45 minutes

Teacher Preparation:
1. Duplicate page 77 for each student.
2. Duplicate a set of the flower patterns on page 76 for each student.
3. Gather the materials listed below.

Materials:
1 copy of page 77 per student
1 copy of the flower patterns per student
1 9" x 12" sheet of construction paper per student
crayons
glue
scissors

Background Information:
   Mother's Day is celebrated on the second Sunday in May. It is observed with gifts of cards, flowers, special breakfasts, and other gestures to honor motherhood.
   Early observances in the United States date back to the 1800s. In 1872, Julia Ward Howe suggested that a special event be held to recognize mothers with a day dedicated to peace. In 1887, Mary Towles Sasseen began conducting her own Mother's Day celebrations. Then, in 1907, Anna Jarvis began to campaign for a national observance of Mother's Day. She also began the tradition of wearing a carnation in honor of the day. Her efforts reached the president, and in 1915, President Woodrow Wilson proclaimed Mother's Day to be recognized annually in May.

Introducing The Lesson:

Tell students that Mother's Day is celebrated on the second Sunday in May. Share the Background Information on page 75 with your students. Explain that flowers have always been an important part of the Mother's Day celebration. Tell students that they will use graphing skills to answer questions about Mother's Day flowers, then create flower-filled cards to give to their mothers (or other special persons).

Steps:

1. Distribute a copy of page 77 to each student. Discuss the information displayed on the bar graph; then have students answer the questions independently.

2. Challenge students to complete the Bonus Box activity.

3. Distribute crayons, scissors, glue, a sheet of construction paper, and a copy of the flower patterns below to each student. Instruct each student to make a card to give as a Mother's Day present.

4. If desired, use the extension activities on page 78 for ideas on student-made gifts to accompany the cards.

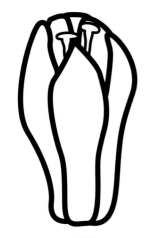

©1997 The Education Center, Inc. • Lifesaver Lessons™ • Grade 3 • TEC500

 # Brilliant Blooms For Mother's Day

Use the graph to answer the following questions.

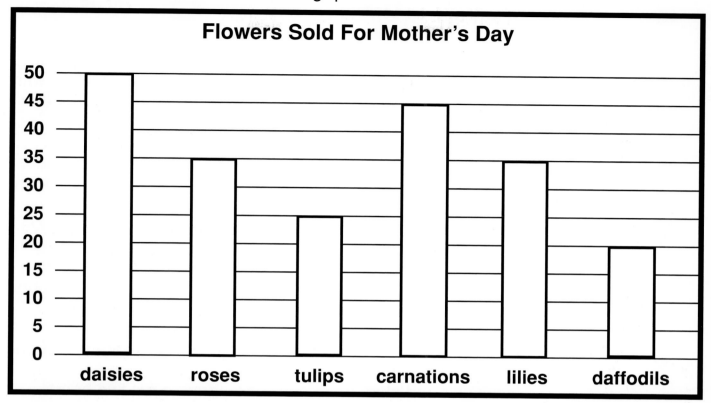

Flowers Sold For Mother's Day

1. How many tulips were sold?_____

2. Which type of flower was sold the most?_____

3. Which type of flower was sold the least?_____

4. Which two flowers were sold the same amount?

_____ and _____

5. How many more carnations than daffodils were sold?_____

6. What is the total number of daisies and carnations sold?_____

7. What is the total number of roses and daffodils sold?_____

8. Daisies sold twice as many as what type of flower?_____

9. Were more carnations or roses sold?_____

10. How many tulips, carnations, and daffodils were sold in all?_____

Bonus Box: How many flowers were sold in all?

©1997 The Education Center, Inc. • *Lifesaver Lessons*™ • Grade 3 • TEC500 • Key p. 95

How To Extend The Lesson:

- Have each student make a self-portrait using crayons or colored pencils. Instruct the student to draw a frame around the portrait. Help each student roll up the completed portrait and secure it with a colorful ribbon. Then have her present it to her mother on Mother's Day.

- These student-made flowery paperweights will add a pretty touch to Mom's desk at work or her dresser at home. Provide each student with a small block of wood and access to old seed and flower catalogs. Instruct each student to cut out pictures of flowers and glue them to all sides of the wood block. After the glue has dried, apply a coat of clear finish to each block and let it dry. Have each student wrap his completed creation in tissue paper and tie it with a ribbon.

- Supply the materials for each student to make a butterfly recipe holder for his mom. Provide each student with a spring-type clothespin, a pair of wiggle eyes, a pipe cleaner, construction paper, markers, scissors, and glue. Instruct each student to cut two heart-shaped pieces from his construction paper. Have him use markers to decorate the shapes with colorful designs. Then show each student how to glue the shapes to the clothespin as shown, creating the butterfly's wings. For a final touch, have the student attach the eyes and pipe-cleaner antennae to the clothespin. If desired, write a recipe on the board for each student to copy on an index card and place in the holder before presenting the gift to his mother.

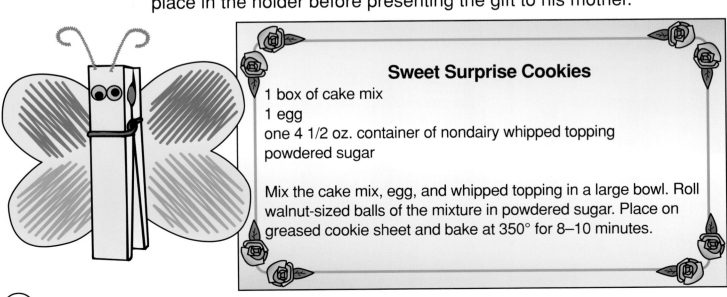

Sweet Surprise Cookies

1 box of cake mix
1 egg
one 4 1/2 oz. container of nondairy whipped topping
powdered sugar

Mix the cake mix, egg, and whipped topping in a large bowl. Roll walnut-sized balls of the mixture in powdered sugar. Place on greased cookie sheet and bake at 350° for 8–10 minutes.

Memorial Day Salute

Pay tribute to Memorial Day with a salute to military ranks and abbreviations.

Skill: Recognizing abbreviations

Estimated Lesson Time: 30 minutes

Teacher Preparation:
1. Duplicate page 81 for each student.
2. Gather the materials listed below.

Materials:
1 copy of page 81 per student
scissors
glue
encyclopedias or other reference books

Background Information:
   Memorial Day is observed on the last Monday in May. The holiday began in 1866 to honor and decorate the graves of Civil War soldiers. Today it is a day to honor military personnel who died while serving the United States. Its original name was Decoration Day because military graves are usually decorated with flowers and flags.
   There are recent additions to Memorial Day activities. Since the end of World War I, volunteers have sold small, red poppies on Memorial Day. (Memorial Day is sometimes referred to as Poppy Day.) The money from these sales helps disabled veterans who have served their country. Many organizations—such as the Boy Scouts, Girl Scouts, and fraternal groups—take part in parades and special programs on Memorial Day. Families visit the graves of all loved ones and bring flowers and wreaths. It is a day when we honor the defenders of our country and remember departed loved ones.

Introducing The Lesson:

Introduce the traditions of Memorial Day by sharing the Background Information on page 79 with your students. Explain that while in recent times people observe the holiday by decorating the graves of all loved ones, the holiday first began in honor of the brave military personnel who defended our country in times of war. Tell students that there are many different ranks of personnel who have served in the United States military, and have the class discuss some of the titles of the different ranks.

Steps:

1. Write the titles shown below on the board. Tell students that the titles are in order of rank. Also explain that different branches of the military have different titles for certain ranks.

2. Write several of the abbreviations on the board. Ask students to match each abbreviation to its title.

3. Distribute a copy of page 81 to each student. Have students complete the activity independently.

4. Challenge students to complete the Bonus Box activity.

Air Force	Army	Marine Corps	Navy
General	General	General	Admiral
Colonel	Colonel	Colonel	Captain
Major	Major	Major	Lieutenant Commander
Captain	Captain	Captain	Lieutenant
First Lieutenant	First Lieutenant	First Lieutenant	Lieutenant Junior
Staff Sergeant	Sergeant	Sergeant	Petty Officer
Airman	Private	Lance Corporal	Seaman

GEN (General)

SGT (Sergeant)

ADM (Admiral)

PVT (Private)

Recognizing abbreviations

Note: Different branches of the military use different capitalization rules for their abbreviations.

Memorial Day Salute

Match each military rank with its correct abbreviation.
Cut out and glue each abbreviation by its rank on the flag.

Gen	LT	MAJ	Sgt	COL	Capt	ADM	LCDR	SR	PO	Amn	Pvt	LCpl

General	Admiral	Colonel	Captain	Major	Lieutenant Commander	Lieutenant	Sergeant	Petty Officer	Airman	Private	Lance Corporal	Seaman Recruit

Note: Different branches of the military use different capitalization rules for their abbreviations.

Bonus Box: Find the name of a famous person in military history. Write his or her name using an abbreviation in the title.

How To Extend The Lesson:

- Create a bulletin-board display of military personnel, medals, and monuments. Encourage your students to contribute pictures of friends and relatives who have served in the armed forces. Tell students to look for Memorial Day features in the newspaper to add to the display as well.

- Invite a veteran or an active-duty military person to come to your class and share information and experiences about the armed forces. If desired, prepare questions ahead of time to send to the person to help steer the discussion.

- Divide your class into groups. Assign each group a different military monument to research and share information about.

- Have your students create poppy pins to distribute to other classrooms. Duplicate copies of the pattern below on red construction paper, or use white paper and have students color the flowers with red crayons. Then have student pairs deliver the poppies and a supply of straight pins to other classes, faculty members, and school volunteers to wear on Memorial Day.

Patterns

©1997 The Education Center, Inc. • *Lifesaver Lessons*™ • Grade 3 • TEC500

Letter-Perfect Dads

Have students use the alphabet to show their fathers 26 reasons that they appreciate them!

Skill: Vocabulary development

Estimated Lesson Time: 45 minutes

Teacher Preparation:
1. Duplicate page 85 for each student.
2. Gather the materials listed below.

Materials:
1 copy of page 85 per student
1 sheet of construction paper per student
crayons or colored pencils
glue
scissors

Background Information:
Father's Day began with an idea from Sonora Louise Smart Dodd of Spokane, Washington. After hearing a sermon on Mother's Day, Ms. Dodd decided that she wanted to honor her father, who had raised six children by himself following the death of his wife. Ms. Dodd drew up a petition to make Father's Day a recognized celebration. On June 19, 1910, the first Father's Day was held in Spokane. Many people continued her efforts to make it a national holiday, and in 1972 President Nixon officially declared the celebration to be held annually on the third Sunday in June.

Introducing The Lesson:

Explain to students the origins of Father's Day as described in the Background Information on page 83. Tell students that Ms. Dodd wanted to honor her father because he was a dedicated father. Write the word *dedicated* on the board. Ask students to list words that describe their fathers (or other special persons). Record their responses on the board.

Steps:

1. Tell students that they are going to use a list of describing words to make cards to present to their fathers on the third Sunday in June.

2. Distribute a copy of page 85 to each student. Explain that each student will write a word to describe his father that begins with each letter on the paper. Remind students to refer to the list on the board if they need help.

3. Have each student cut out his completed list on the lines. Demonstrate how to glue the list to the inside of a folded sheet of construction paper as shown below.

4. Have each student decorate the front of his card.

5. If desired use the extension activities on page 86 for Father's Day gift ideas. Have each student attach his card to the gift before presenting it to his father.

Letter-Perfect Dads

Write a word that describes your father for each letter of the alphabet.
Then cut out the list and follow your teacher's directions to make a card.

To A Letter-Perfect Dad

A_____   H_____

B_____   I_____

C_____   J_____

D_____   K_____

E_____   L_____

F_____   M_____

G_____

N_____   T_____

O_____   U_____

P_____   V_____

Q_____   W_____

R_____   X_____

S_____   Y_____

                   Z_____

Love, _____

How To Extend The Lesson:

• Give each student a paper lunch sack and a supply of the pattern below. Have each student write a special message to her father on each pattern, then place the patterns in the bag. If desired have each student decorate her sack before presenting her father with a bagful of special messages.

• Have students create special coupon books for their fathers or special persons. Provide each student with a piece of green construction paper cut into dollar-bill-size sections. Instruct each student to draw a dollar sign in the corner of each section and write "You're Priceless!" across the front. Then have each student program the back of each bill with a chore or special favor he will do for his father. Staple the bills into a coupon booklet for each student to give to his father.

• Send students packing as they prepare a pretend trip to give to their fathers on Father's Day. Have each student select a destination he would like to travel to with his father. Then have the student create a travel brochure listing sights and activities for the chosen place. For an added touch, have each student draw a suitcase outline on a sheet of construction paper and fill the suitcase with magazine cutouts showing the items that they will need on their trip. Provide an envelope for each student to use to wrap the brochure and suitcase surprise.

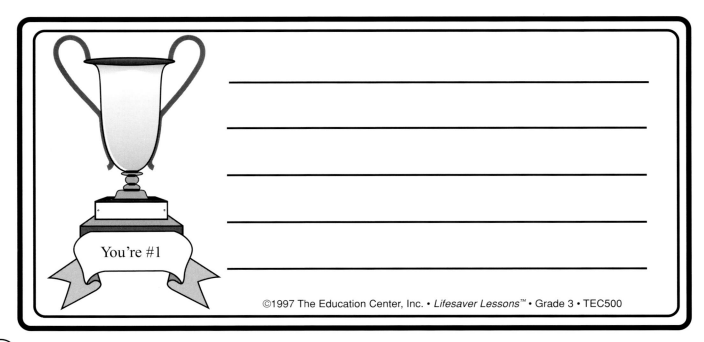

You're #1

©1997 The Education Center, Inc. • *Lifesaver Lessons*™ • Grade 3 • TEC500

Patriotic Proofreading

*Reinforce important concepts about independence
while reviewing sentence-writing skills.*

 Skill: Using correct capitalization and punctuation

 Estimated Lesson Time: 45 minutes

Teacher Preparation:
Duplicate a copy of page 89 for each student.

Materials:
1 copy of page 89 per student

Teacher Reference:
Independence Day was considered by our forefathers as a time for rejoicing. John Adams declared, "I am apt to believe that it will be celebrated by succeeding generations as the great anniversary festival…It ought to be solemnized with pomp and parade, with shows, games, sports, guns, bells, bonfires, and illuminations, from one end of this continent to the other, from this time forward for evermore." John Adams's predictions have proven correct!

Introducing The Lesson:

Tell students that the most important summer holiday is celebrated on July 4, in honor of our country's independence. Ask students to name items associated with Independence Day celebrations. List the responses on the board.

Steps:

1. Ask student volunteers to use the items listed to compose a sentence. Have each volunteer dictate her sentence as you write it on the board—but do not use any capital letters or punctuation as you write.

2. After you have recorded a desired number of sentences on the board, have your students identify the errors in capitalization and punctuation. Call on students to come to the board to make the necessary corrections.

3. Distribute a copy of page 89 to each student. Tell students that they will look for errors in the statements about Independence Day.

4. After your students have completed the reproducible, challenge them to complete the Bonus Box activity.

fireworks
picnics
flags
red, white, and blue
parades
stars

we have a picnic on independence day
there are a lot of colorful fireworks
we put our flag by our front door
sometimes we watch floats in a parade

Patriotic Proofreading

Read the following sentences.
Find and correct the mistakes in capitalization and punctuation.
Rewrite the sentences.
The firecracker will tell you how many of each type of mistake
  to correct in each sentence.

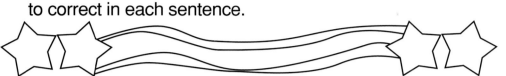

capitals   punctuation

1. independence day is america's birthday

2. did you know that it's a celebration of freedom

3. we declared freedom on july 2 1776

4. two days later we signed the declaration of independence

5. we celebrate the day it was signed

6. people used to celebrate by firing guns and cannons

7. don't you think that sounds dangerous

8. today, people have parades picnics and special music

9. some cities have fireworks displays

10. what do you do on independence day

Bonus Box: How many words can you spell using the letters in the word *Independence?*
Write them on the back of this paper.

89

©1997 The Education Center, Inc. • *Lifesaver Lessons*™ • Grade 3 • TEC500 • Key p. 95

How To Extend The Lesson:

- Have each student make a poster to commemorate our independence. Supply each student with a sheet of construction paper and access to red, white, and blue paints. Display patriotic symbols for students to refer to as they design their posters.

- Discuss the ways in which people show their patriotic feelings. Inform students that one important form of expression is through song. Familiarize your students with recordings of patriotic tunes such as "Yankee Doodle," "America," "The Star-Spangled Banner," and "This Land Is Your Land."

- Place students into small groups to research symbols of America. Instruct each group to choose a symbol such as the American flag, the bald eagle, the Statue of Liberty, the Washington Monument, or Uncle Sam. Have each group discover five facts about its symbol, then present their findings to the class.

- To help students understand the concept of independence, challenge them to consider what the idea might mean to different people. What freedoms would a six-year-old hope to have? A sixteen-year-old? A sixty-year-old? What freedoms do your students have at home that would not work well at school? Then have each student write his own definition of independence.

- Salute the red, white, and blue with these patriotic literature selections:
  —*The Glorious Fourth At Prairietown* by Joan Anderson (Morrow Junior Books, 1986)
  —*Happy Birthday, America* by Marsha Chall (Lothrop, Lee & Shepard Books; 1997)
  —*A Fourth Of July On The Plains* by Jean Van Leeuwen (Dial Books For Young Readers, 1996)
  —*Independence Day* by Wilma W. Gore (Enslo Publishers, Inc.; 1993)

A Rainbow Of Friends

Celebrate Friendship Day with this self-esteem-boosting activity.

Skill: Following directions

Estimated Lesson Time: 30 minutes

Teacher Preparation:
1. Duplicate a copy of page 93 for each student.
2. Write each student's name on a separate slip of paper. Place the slips in a container.
3. Gather the supplies listed below.

Materials:
1 copy of page 93 per student
1 sheet of blue construction paper per student
crayons or colored pencils
scissors
glue
slips of paper programmed with students' names
container

Background Information:
Friendship Day is celebrated on August 2. The celebration was suggested by Joyce C. Hall, the founder of Hallmark® Cards, and it was decreed by Congress in 1935.

Introducing The Lesson:

Tell students that August 2 is a day for people to celebrate friendship. Ask students to name some qualities of being a good friend while you record their responses on the board. Then explain that each student will randomly select the name of a classmate and list qualities that make that person a good friend.

Steps:

1. Have each student take a slip of paper from the container. Ask each student not to reveal the name she selected. (Make sure that a student does not draw her own name.)

2. Distribute a copy of page 93 and a sheet of blue construction paper to each student.

3. Instruct each student to write the name from her slip of paper on the cloud. Then, in each stripe of the rainbow, have the student list a quality about the person that makes her a good friend.

4. Instruct each student to carefully color the rainbow so that the words are not obscured. Then have each student cut out the rainbow and glue it to the construction paper.

5. Display the completed projects on a bulletin board and invite students to read what their classmates have written about them.

Name _____

Write a friend's name on the cloud.
On each stripe of the rainbow,
   tell why that person is
   a good friend.

©1997 The Education Center, Inc. • *Lifesaver Lessons*™ • Grade 3 • TEC500

Note To The Teacher: Use with the activity on page 92.

How To Extend The Lesson:

• Have students work in pairs to create friendship collages. Instruct each student to interview his partner to find out likes, dislikes, interests, and hobbies. Then have each student create a collage about his partner using phrases, drawings, and pictures from magazines.

• Decorate your classroom in honor of Friendship Day with a friendship chain. Write the name of each student on a separate strip of construction paper. Then randomly distribute a strip of paper to each student. Instruct each student to write a positive message about his classmate on the paper. Assemble the chain by making a link from each strip and gluing its ends together.

• Create a tasty friendship snack by asking each student to bring in an ingredient for fruit salad. Help students wash and cut up the fruit; then have students work together to combine the ingredients and place portions into bowls for all to enjoy.

• Share stories about friendships with your students from this collection of books:

—*Amber Brown Is Not A Crayon* by Paula Danziger (G. P. Putnam's Sons, 1994)
—*Hey, New Kid!* by Betsy Duffey (Viking Children's Books, 1996)
—*Ellen Tebbits* by Beverly Cleary (Morrow Junior Books, 1951)
—*A Weekend With Wendell* by Kevin Henkes (Greenwillow Books, 1986)
—*Best Friends For Francis* by Russell Hoban (HarperCollins Children's Books, 1976)
—*Charlotte's Web* by E. B. White (HarperCollins Children's Books, 1952)

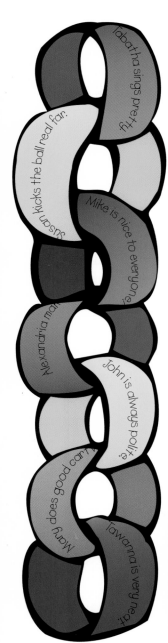

Lindsey
She helps me with math.

Answer Keys

Page 25
1. red
2. red
3. orange
4. orange
5. orange
6. red
7. red
8. orange
9. orange
10. orange
11. red
12. red

Page 33
1. boxes, ribbons
2. matches, candles
3. wishes, toys
4. lights, inches
5. benches, skates
6. branches, trees
7. bells, churches
8. kisses, gifts
9. patches, boots
10. glasses, pieces

Page 53
1. President Lincoln
2. President Roosevelt
3. President Tyler
4. President Roosevelt
5. Presidents Madison and Eisenhower
6. 8 years
7. President Tyler
8. Presidents Washington and Lincoln
9. 16th
10. 1953–61

Page 77
1. 25
2. daisies
3. daffodils
4. roses and lilies
5. 25
6. 95
7. 55
8. tulips
9. carnations
10. 90
Bonus Box: 210

Page 81
General—Gen
Admiral—ADM
Colonel—COL
Captain—Capt
Major—MAJ
Lieutenant Commander—LCDR
Lieutenant—LT
Sergeant—Sgt
Petty Officer—PO
Airman—Amn
Private—Pvt
Lance Corporal—LCpl
Seaman Recruit—SR

Page 89
1. Independence Day is America's birthday.
2. Did you know that it's a celebration of freedom?
3. We declared freedom on July 2, 1776.
4. Two days later we signed the Declaration of Independence.
5. We celebrate the day it was signed.
6. People used to celebrate by firing guns and cannons.
7. Don't you think that sounds dangerous?
8. Today, people have parades, picnics, and special music.
9. Some cities have fireworks displays.
10. What do you do on Independence Day?

Grade 3 Holidays & Celebrations Management Checklist

HOLIDAYS & CELEBRATIONS	PAGES	COMMENTS
NATIONAL GRANDPARENTS DAY	3	
NATIVE AMERICAN DAY	7	
COLUMBUS DAY	11	
UNITED NATIONS DAY	15	
HALLOWEEN	19	
THANKSGIVING	23	
HANUKKAH	27	
CHRISTMAS	31	
KWANZAA	35	
MARTIN LUTHER KING, JR. DAY	39	
CHINESE NEW YEAR	43	
VALENTINE'S DAY	47	
PRESIDENTS' DAY	51	
ST. PATRICK'S DAY	55	
EASTER	59	
INTERNATIONAL CHILDREN'S BOOK DAY	63	
EARTH DAY	67	
CINCO DE MAYO	71	
MOTHER'S DAY	75	
MEMORIAL DAY	79	
FATHER'S DAY	83	
INDEPENDENCE DAY	87	
FRIENDSHIP DAY	91	

©1997 The Education Center, Inc. • *Lifesaver Lessons*™ • Grade 3 • TEC500